Developing Creative Leadership

Developing Creative Leadership

Jeanette Plauché Parker
and
Lucy Gremillion Regnaud

TEACHER IDEAS PRESS
Portsmouth, NH

Teacher Ideas Press
A division of Reed Elsevier Inc.
361 Hanover Street
Portsmouth, NH 03801–3912
www.teacherideaspress.com

Offices and agents throughout the world

The author and publisher wish to thank those who have generously given permission to reprint borrowed material:

"Lost on the Moon" simulation adapted by permission of Dr. Jay Hall.

"Creative Problem Solving" diagram from www.creativelearning.com is reprinted by permission of Don Treffinger.

Library of Congress Cataloging-in-Publication Data

Parker, Jeanette Plauche.
    Developing creative leadership / Jeanette Plauche Parker and Lucy Gremillion Begnaud.
      p. cm. — (Gifted treasury series)
    ISBN 1-56308-631-X
    1. Gifted children-Education. 2. Leadership-Study and teaching. I.
Begnaud, Lucy Gremillion. II. Title. III. Series.
    LC3993.2 .P37 2003 *2004*
    371.95—dc22   2003015325

Editor: Suzanne Barchers
Production Coordinator: Angela Laughlin
Typesetter: Westchester Book Services
Cover design: Joni Doherty
Manufacturing: Steve Bernier

Printed in the United States of America on acid-free paper

08 07 06 05 04 VP 1 2 3 4 5

Contents

Acknowledgments

As with any work of value, this project depended on the assistance of numerous friends, colleagues, authors, and others. Although it is not possible to name all who influenced its development, I would like to acknowledge certain individuals who contributed directly to the production of the final manuscript. Clearly the most influential was my husband, George Parker, who continues to encourage my professional involvement. I must also acknowledge my mentor, Dr. E. Paul Torrance, for the lasting influence he has had on every creative work I have produced, and my friend and colleague Frances Karnes, a recognized authority on leadership development, for her continued encouragement of my work over the years.

In the production of the current project, I gratefully acknowledge the assistance of Tom Spencer, formerly a graduate student in our master's program in gifted education, who took an interest in my proposed project and voluntarily undertook the initial screening of instructional units for this book. I am also indebted to my secretary and close friend Brenda Mark for her many contributions to everything I produce, and to my graduate assistant Rebekah Granger Ellis, who assisted me greatly in locating references for the final editing of my manuscript. I also would like to acknowledge my many former graduate students who have espoused the cause of leadership development and adopted my *Leadership Training Model* in their gifted classes. Finally, I must give credit to the administration of our university: Dr. Ray Authement, President; Dr. Steve Landry, Academic Vice President; and Dr. Gerald Carlson, Dean of Education, for their continued encouragement and support for all of our efforts in gifted education. Without their help, this project would not have been possible.

Jeanette Plauché Parker

Many people have assisted in the completion of this book. My primary appreciation goes to my family. My husband, Gerald P. Begnaud, Jr. is my best friend, my confidante, and my biggest fan. My children, Barbara and Geoff, unselfishly inspire me when I need a lift. Words cannot express my gratefulness to dear friends Betty Laperouse and Robin Picheloup, who consistently lent their love and support. I am in awe of their patience with me! My parents, brothers, sisters, and mother-in-law encouraged me as I continued on my journey. Dora Johnson, my secretary and friend, was my sounding board and my assistant throughout this process. Certainly, this book could not have been written without the input from students who submitted units. It was difficult to determine which units would be placed in this book, and I appreciate the extra efforts of those writers whose units were chosen. A special thank you to Jeanette Parker, who saw my leadership abilities long before I did. She continues to be my mentor and my friend. Final appreciation goes to all of my students over the years who have made teaching a pleasure for me. I continue to learn from them daily. Hopefully, the leadership skills I have nurtured in them will serve them well in the future. I suspect that is what it is all about.

Lucy Gremillion Begnaud

Preface

Since the beginning of written history (and perhaps even earlier), human beings have recognized the need for leadership. Although few modern thinkers still espouse Aristotle's theory that "From the hours of their birth, some are marked out for subjugation and others for command," the basic attributes and tasks of effective leadership have remained much the same.

Essentially the literature acknowledges four theories of leadership. Perhaps the oldest of these is the Trait Theory, to which Aristotle subscribed—the notion that "leaders are born and not made." A second theory of leadership is the Position Theory—the idea that any person placed in a leadership position (or a position with power) is a leader. The Style Theory simply proposes that leaders utilize three styles of leadership—Autocratic ("Do as I say"), Democratic ("Let's do this together"), and Laissez-Faire ("Do whatever you want to do"). Finally, the Distributed Functions Theory (also called Situational Leadership) suggests that different individuals will assume leadership roles according to the contexts or domains in which their talents prevail.

In *Leading Minds* (1995), an excellent synthesis of the similarities among recognized leaders such as Eleanor Roosevelt, Winston Churchill, and Martin Luther King, Jr., Howard Gardner observed that there are two modes of leadership: direct and indirect. Indirect leaders set examples through their work. These are the Beethovens, the Einsteins, the Renoirs—individuals who come to be recognized as leaders because of the innovative and exemplary nature of their contributions to and within their own domains of endeavor. Direct leaders, on the other hand, become the CEOs of large corporations, the dynamic leaders of nations, the presidents of major organizations. While direct and indirect leadership need not be mutually exclusive (i.e., direct leaders can lead indirectly through their writings, and indirect leaders can assume positions of direct leadership through their involvement in professional organizations), it is direct leadership that has the greatest potential for development through the educational system. It is therefore this goal that will be addressed herein.

Like the Trait Theory, the Position Theory must be discarded if we believe that leadership ability can be developed. John Gardner (1990) cautions against equating status, power, or authority with leadership. Status frequently results from election to a high position; however, any study of history will identify many persons placed in high positions who were totally ineffective as leaders. With regard to power or authority, consider the special interest group that contributes heavily to a political campaign, the IRS agent who audits your tax return, the traffic officer who stops you on the highway for a broken taillight. All of these people or groups wield power through authority. But that power does not in itself make them leaders. Reflect similarly on the political leaders of our lifetime, and it will quickly become apparent that appointment or even election to a lofty and important position does not automatically effect leadership.

When considering leadership styles, one might suggest that Adolf Hitler was the consummate example of an autocratic leader. Hitler commanded a huge assemblage of followers who saw him as highly charismatic and persuasive. As a result, he easily accomplished many of his goals. But what a disaster his leadership imposed on the world! Laissez-faire leaders, on the other hand, may be popular among their special-interest constituencies, but they rarely succeed in either accomplishing effective followership or the achievement of worthy group goals. There can be little doubt that democratic leadership is the most effective, and certainly the most desirable and productive, approach. John Gardner (1990) emphasized the usefulness of *leadership teams*—groups that work together, sharing the leadership role as various needs arise. As he observed, leaders such as Truman and Kennedy had a unique talent for surrounding themselves with persons of extraordinary talent. It was that talent—the ability to build solid leadership teams—that enabled them and others like them to be so highly effective.

The Theory of Situational Leadership (or the Distributed Functions Theory) may hold the greatest promise in the context of leadership development. In combination with a democratic style and the use of leadership teams, this approach offers the benefits derived from the availability and use of expertise in the numerous areas involved in the reaching of any goal, the solving of any problem, or the achievement of any other group effort. If we wish to prepare today's "brightest and best" students for effective citizenship in the twenty-first century, we must help them to develop the skills that will enable and empower them to assume leadership roles that match their individual domains of talent.

When I began studying the place of leadership development in the curriculum, I discovered that the field of education was sadly deficient in this important methodology. Consulting the literature on the strategies that run business and industry, I concluded that the skills required for effective leadership fell into four major areas, which I classify as *Cognition, Problem Solving, Interpersonal Communication,* and *Decision Making*. It is on this theory that the *Leadership Training Model* is based.

One final statement should be made regarding the perspectives presented in this book: The philosophy underlying the *Leadership Training Model* does not imply that only the intellectually gifted have the ability to lead. In reality, many of history's most effective leaders (both direct and indirect) would have failed to qualify for today's programs for gifted students. Albert Einstein and Thomas Edison are familiar examples of scientific giants who in their early lives were perceived as limited in ability and promise. Frequently I am asked the question, "Should teachers of the gifted be gifted?" We might, then, ask in similar fashion, "Must leaders be gifted?" My response to both of these questions is, "Absolutely . . . as long as giftedness is defined appropriately!" And how should we define giftedness in these contexts? Renzulli (1978, 1986) theorizes that giftedness (or gifted behavior) exists when three traits are present in interaction: above-average intelligence, creative ability, and task commitment. It is my contention that this interaction—in combination with the requisite skills—is essential for effective leadership. With this assertion in mind, then, the use of the *Leadership Training Model* should not be limited to the gifted program; it is appropriate and useful for all classrooms.

Jeanette Plauché Parker

Organization of the Book

In keeping with our philosophy that programs for the gifted should be based on a leadership training perspective, the first section of this book presents an overview of the literature on leadership, followed by a discussion of the *Leadership Training Model (LTM),* a comprehensive model on which gifted programs may be based. Suggestions are made for developing programs around the model, and specific strategies are suggested for developing each of the four primary components that make up its structure. Following each chapter in the first section is a list of additional resources that provide activities germane to the strategies discussed in the text.

The second section of the book presents a selection of instructional units based on the *LTM* that can be adopted (or adapted) for developing leadership potential in a variety of subject areas across the full spectrum of elementary and secondary schools. These units have been developed over the years by graduate students in our gifted education classes, and modified as needed to fit the needs of this project. We are most grateful to these students for granting us permission to include their outstanding products in this publication, and we trust that their work will be equally appreciated by those teachers who use it in their classes.

One final comment should be made with respect to the form of writing used in this book. In recent years, considerable attention has been given to the need to avoid gender-specific language in publication. Although these efforts are admirable, indiscriminately selected phraseology frequently results in material that interrupts the reader's continuity of thought. In order to enhance the readability of the book while adhering to currently preferred trends, we have chosen to alternate by chapter the use of masculine and feminine pronouns and their adjectival forms in circumstances in which the gender is either unknown or irrelevant.

Developing Creative Leadership

PART I

Perspectives on Leadership

Introduction

Most men and women go through their lives
using no more than a fraction . . .
of the potentialities within them.
The reservoir of unused human talent and energy
is vast,
and learning to tap that reservoir more effectively
is one of the exciting tasks ahead for humankind. . . .
Among the untapped capabilities are leadership gifts.

(Gardner, 1990, p. xv)

Aristotle is said to have believed that *from the hour of their birth some are marked out for subjugation and others for command*. In today's pluralistic society, which acknowledges the many types of ability possessed by human beings, the outmoded Trait Theory—the belief that *leaders are born and not made*—has long been regarded as a fallacy.

Early in the last decade of the twentieth century, President George H. Bush began talking about "leadership for a new world order." With the fall of the Berlin Wall, the division of Yugoslavia, the dissolution of the Soviet Union, and other dramatic events, the world was undergoing drastic changes. John F. Kennedy's prophetic statement had come to pass: "It is time for a new generation of leadership to cope with new problems and new opportunities. For there is a new world to be won." Our national leaders began to recognize new challenges in the need for leadership of a new era. As Alvin Toffler observed, it is erroneous to think that a style of leadership that worked in the past could work in the present, much less the future. Just as the world has progressed from the Industrial Revolution (which Toffler labeled the "second wave" of civilization) to the age of technology (or Toffler's "third wave"), there must be a Leadership Revolution—the development of leadership at all levels: people who think differently, who value and respect diversity, and who are committed to creating a new and different kind of future (Morse, 1991).

It is unfortunate that, while leaders at all levels have cited the need for leadership, the void continues to exist. It is time for our educational systems to fill this void.

Jeanette Plauché Parker

Chapter One

What Is Leadership?

The term "leadership" has been defined in many ways. According to Howard Gardner (1995), President Harry Truman saw a leader as a person who could "get other people to do what they don't want to do and like it." Similarly, Eileen Ford, cofounder of the Ford model agency, defines leadership as "the ability to convince people that they want to do what you want them to do as if they had thought of it themselves" (Karnes & Bean, 1993). Leadership guru Warren Bennis sees leadership as "the energetic process of getting other people fully and willingly committed to a course of action, to meet commonly agreed objectives." He further states that leadership is about "understanding people" and connecting with potential followers, as well as "having a unique vision, making strategic choices, and designing and enabling an organization to get the job done" (Yates, 2002). John Gardner (1990), however, emphasizes that leadership is only one of many roles fulfilled by members of groups, and that the function of the leader is to perform those tasks that are essential for the accomplishment of the group's goals.

Current theories of leadership tend to lean toward "horizontal" models of leadership—leadership styles that emphasize collaboration and teamwork. Noting that centralized authority cannot adequately meet the leadership needs of large organizations, Gardner (1990) suggests that all individuals must be prepared to assume leadership roles and tasks as the situation dictates. He emphasizes the importance of leadership teams, which tend to foster feelings of ownership and pride in the overall product of their endeavors, and calls to mind examples such as Truman and Kennedy, who surrounded themselves with capable individuals who lent their individual talents for the good of the whole and helped their presidents to become exceptional leaders.

In *Leading Minds* (1995), Howard Gardner distinguishes between direct and indirect leadership. Indirect leaders—the Einsteins, the Mozarts, the Renoirs—are those who lead by example within their specific disciplines or "domains of expertise." These creative geniuses may never provide *direct* leadership—working with and leading groups in the active pursuit of specific goals; nonetheless they are viewed as leaders in their fields, in that they set standards, by example, for others to follow. Indirect leadership is a highly individual quality; only a small number of persons in a given area of endeavor will demonstrate this type of leadership. Direct leadership, on the other hand, is the task of presidents, CEOs, committee chairs, and others who have the responsibility for leading others in the deliberate pursuit of specific goals. Gardner (1990) further distinguishes between leadership and other qualities such as status (e.g. presidents who were highly intelligent but totally ineffective at leading our nation), power (e.g., dictators such as Adolph Hitler), and authority (e.g., IRS auditors).

It is no longer possible to lead by adhering strictly to the status quo; continuous renewal must take place (Gardner, 1990). To realize this goal, we must act boldly to *escape* the present and look toward the future. It is widely acknowledged that human beings use only a small portion of their abilities, and—according to Gardner—these include leadership talents. Gardner further postulates that *leadership can be taught*—that most of the skills that enable a person to be an effective leader are learned rather than inborn. Although there is unquestionably a dire need to mold attitudes and develop diverse potentials throughout society, we must begin to develop leadership in the early years. It is the moral and professional obligation of schools and teachers to prepare our young people for effective citizenship as society's future adults. Obviously not all of the current generation of students will become leaders in tomorrow's society. But, as Gardner observed, we can produce a "substantial cadre of young potential leaders from which the next generation of leaders will emerge" (p. 162).

Regardless of which theory or definition we espouse, we must acknowledge that leadership involves both conceptual knowledge and skill. If we are to maximize the leadership potentials of our gifted youth, we must identify those concepts and skills and seek to develop them through appropriately differentiated strategies. In reviewing the research on leadership, I find a clear dichotomy for classifying leadership skills; as with most other areas of education, these skills can easily be grouped into two broad areas or domains: cognitive leadership and affective leadership. The brief discussion that follows summarizes the traits, concepts, and skills that comprise effective leadership in these two essential domains.

COGNITIVE LEADERSHIP

Creative and Critical Thinking

When I was preparing for my doctoral comprehensive examination, one professor gave me a take-home question, forewarning me that he did not know the answer! The question, which sounded rather simple at first glance, was, "Is creativity a cognitive process?"

Having cut my gifted education teeth on the concept of hemispheric laterality—the theory that logic is controlled by the left side of the brain and creativity by the right—my first impulse was to answer *no*. However, as I researched the cognitive psychology writings of Dewey, Ausubel, and others, I became convinced that creativity was indeed a cognitive process. It is not within the scope of this book to explore this argument to any depth; however, it was this research that motivated me to classify creativity along with logic under cognitive leadership.

A brief glance at the problem-solving process will show that it requires alternating between convergence and divergence (see, for example, Treffinger, Isaksen, & Dorval, 1994). Logical thinking is required when analyzing the facts of a situation and diagnosing the nature of the problem—the problem-finding step that is so essential to good problem solving. It is also used in the process of evaluating alternatives generated through brainstorming, and in creating the final plan for solving the problem. Creative thinking, on the other hand, is essential to produce innovative ideas and to complete the "troubleshooting" that must precede the actual implementation of a solution. Contrary to popular opinion, logical thinking and creative thinking actually complement one another!

Some leadership characteristics that are related to creativity include **visualization** (not only having insight, innovative ideas, and vision, but also being able to communicate the vision and to visualize its realization), **ability to withhold judgment** (resisting temptation to evaluate ideas before examining them, and openness to new ideas), **flexibility** (the ability to adapt to changing circumstances—an essential characteristic of an effective leader), **resourcefulness** (knowledge of human, technological, and economic resources that are available for help in solving problems), **willingness to take risks** (the ability to think divergently and give up the status quo through a commitment to productive change), and **problem-solving ability** (the ability to identify and solve problems in both creative and logical ways). Karnes & Zimmerman (2001) cite the ability to solve problems creatively, and effective problem solvers must be able to think divergently with a long-term perspective, having the ability to see where their solutions fit into the larger context of real life.

Futuristic Thinking

Alvin Toffler, author of *Future Shock* and *Third Wave,* cited a need to develop in our future leaders a "future-focused role image." Frequently, gifted children—particularly those from economically disadvantaged homes—have difficulty imaging a positive future for themselves. A positive future image is essential for potential leaders. While the attitudinal aspect of the future-focused role image may be considered affective, the development of that attitude through future problem solving and other future studies techniques is decidedly cognitive.

Knowledge and Skills of Search

The preceding discussion presented three types of thinking that are essential for effective cognitive leadership—creative thinking, logical (or critical) thinking, and futuristic thinking. John Dewey is said to have remarked, "We can have facts without thinking, but we cannot have thinking without facts." As teachers, we must acknowledge that the knowledge explosion has made it impossible for us to recognize—much less know or teach—all the facts that today's students will need as tomorrow's leaders. But without a thorough understanding of a situation, a leader cannot be effective. No one can know everything, but much can be gained through efficient skills of search. As a background for any effective effort, a leader must possess above-average intelligence and a broad knowledge about many subjects, with a firm grounding in the disciplines.

AFFECTIVE LEADERSHIP

Affective leadership depends on the possession (and/or the development) of affective skills that facilitate the accomplishment of the tasks for which leaders are chosen. Essentially, affective leadership can be divided into three components: personal attributes, interpersonal communication skills, and decision-making skills.

Personal Attributes

While most thinking people see the fallacy in Aristotle's Trait Theory, it is apparent that certain personal attributes contribute to one's effectiveness as a leader. Perhaps the most important of these attributes is a belief in oneself. As Martin Luther King, Jr. observed, we must first teach students to believe in themselves (Gardner, 1990). Other important attributes that can be developed are enthusiasm, genuineness, independence and self-directedness, and task commitment. Leaders must be willing to take risks and become pioneers. To become pioneers, they must be self-confident, assertive, and dynamic. Also essential are goal orientation (with the ability to evaluate on the basis of realistic goals), organizational skills, and an almost fanatical drive for quality.

Interpersonal Communication Skills

Piaget observed that very young children are egocentric, viewing the world as if they were at its center. On the basis of his developmental theory, social education begins with the family, branching out gradually to the neighborhood, the community, the state, the nation, and finally the world. So it is with interpersonal communication. Until self-understanding is established, the individual cannot reach out to (much less communicate effectively with) others.

Like human development, interpersonal communication skills are hierarchical—they must be developed in sequence. The first stage in this development is **self-awareness**, built through self-exploration and reflection as the individual begins to understand self. Until self-understanding is achieved, **self-confidence** will not develop. Abraham Maslow saw self-actualization as the ultimate goal of human effort, and Lawrence Kohlberg placed human actions on a continuum of moral development. "Self-actualizing" persons would likely be operating at Kohlberg's highest level of moral development, motivated by an inner locus of control, acting from their own motivations rather than worrying about other people's judgment. Self-confidence must be achieved before one can begin to reach out to others.

Gardner (1990) has observed that leaders not only must have confidence in their own ability but also must be able to communicate that confidence. In the words of Clarence Randall (1964), "The leader must know, must know that he knows, and must be able to make it abundantly clear to those about him that he knows." Carl Rogers, well known for his work in the area of humanistic psychology and education, pointed out the importance of **empathy** and genuineness. It was probably Rogers from whom the gifted education movement took its emphasis on the teacher as facilitator. The effective leader must be willing to listen and respond to the concerns and needs of others. Until empathy is achieved, the **ability to communicate with others** will be stifled. Leaders must respect and encourage others, inspiring confidence in their effort to lead the group in the right direction and facilitating the group process without dictating. Finally, when the ability to communicate effectively on an interpersonal level is achieved, people can be **empowered** to make decisions and solve problems. Groups that are empowered by their leaders feel significant in their group roles, accept failures as learning experiences, see their work as exciting and important, and consider themselves part of a community (Bennis, 1989).

Other qualities and skills that are essential in developing effective interpersonal skills are the ability to delegate responsibility, manage the work and time of others, and facilitate teamwork. The leader must be able to motivate others, to foster creative production, and to respect diversity among the members of the team.

Decision-Making Skills

Finally, effective leaders must possess decision-making skills: high moral and ethical standards and the courage to stand up for their convictions, the willingness to accept responsibility, the judicious use of authority, and the ability to evaluate—at the appropriate time. Leaders must be decisive and able to reach both rational and creative solutions, to earn and be able to hold the trust of others. Finally, the effective leader must have a strong motivation to excel.

LEADERSHIP IN GIFTED EDUCATION:

The Leadership Training Model

Early in my career as a gifted education specialist, I concluded that leadership development should be the major goal of programs for our "brightest and best" youth. Warren Bennis (1989) maintained that even though President Jimmy Carter had "more facts at his fingertips than almost any other president," he "never made the meaning come through the facts." According to Bennis, leaders must "communicate their vision"—make their ideas real to those they lead. Ideas that are not understood will not be supported. In Bennis's words, ". . . no matter how marvelous the vision, the effective leader must use a metaphor, a word, or a model to make that vision clear to others" (p. 14). Our brightest youngsters have the intellectual potential to be our most effective leaders; however, much human talent remains undeveloped. It is therefore critical for our schools to develop the latent potentials of our gifted students. It is also essential that we strive for **integrative** leadership—leadership that blends cognitive skills and knowledge with affective traits and processes. Only by using an integrative approach to leadership development can we hope to produce gifted leaders for the future of our nation and "the new world order."

Suzanne Morse (1991) pointed out that "Our world is so complex, interdependent, and interrelated that the old paradigms of singular leadership will not work and cannot work. Just as the world moved from the industrial revolution to the technological, there must be a leadership revolution" (p. 3). I believe that Morse's contention applies to gifted education as well. Programs for gifted and talented youth utilize a wide variety of models; however, if we are to prepare tomorrow's leaders for the twenty-first century, we must develop **new** paradigms. In his prophetic book *Third Wave,* Toffler (1980) observed that today's educational systems are a throwback to the industrial revolution, when the primary goal of schools was to prepare people to work in factories! We are no longer in an industrial revolution; we are immersed in the "third wave" of civilization—the age of information and technology. What worked in the past will not work for the future. We *must* develop new paradigms if our world is to succeed. As Torrance observed,

> Democracies collapse . . . when they fail to use intelligent, imaginative methods for solving their problems. Greece failed to heed such a warning by Socrates and gradually collapsed (1962, p. 6).

On the basis of the research on leadership, I have proposed a model for development of "integrative leadership" in the gifted and talented. The *Leadership Training Model* (1983, 1989) identifies four primary components of leadership within cognitive and affective structures—*Cognition* and *Problem Solving* on the cognitive (perhaps "left-brain") side, and *Interpersonal Communication* and *Decision Making* on the affective ("right-brain") side. The section that follows discusses these components in some detail and presents suggestions and strategies for utilizing the model as a foundation for gifted programs.

ADDITIONAL RESOURCES

Flack, J. D. (1997). *From the land of enchantment: Creative teaching with fairy tales* (pp. 89–133). Englewood, CO: Teacher Ideas Press.

Flack, J. D. (1993). I is for invention. In *Talent Ed: Strategies for developing the talent in every learner* (pp. 97–103). Englewood, CO: Teacher Ideas Press.

Flack, J. D. (1989). *Inventing, inventions, and inventors: A teaching resource book* (pp. 106–127). Englewood, CO: Teacher Ideas Press.

Flack, J. D. (1990). *Mystery and detection: Thinking and problem solving with the sleuths* (pp. 141–166). Englewood, CO: Teacher Ideas Press.

Flack, J. D. (1993). *Talent Ed: Strategies for developing the talent in every learner* (p. 83). Englewood, CO: Teacher Ideas Press.

Polette, N. (2000). *Gifted books, gifted readers: Literature activities to excite young minds.* Englewood, CO: Teacher Ideas Press.

Chapter Two

Developing Gifted Leadership for the New Millennium

> . . . education of the gifted and talented for leadership
> involves not only the development of unusual potential
> but the values, the concern, the motivation to use those special talents
> for the benefit of society.
>
> A. Harry Passow

In the quarter of a century since the 1972 publication of Commissioner Sidney Marland's landmark report to the U.S. Congress, much progress has been made in the offering of differentiated educational opportunities for our nation's gifted and talented youth. In its *2001–2002 State of the States Gifted and Talented Education Report* (in press), the Council of State Directors of Programs for the Gifted reported that twenty-nine states mandate and/or fund gifted programs, twenty-nine have professional certification or endorsement for teachers of the gifted, and twenty-one states employ at least one full-time state director of gifted education. The *2003–2004 Directory of Graduate Degree Programs and Services in Gifted and Talented Education* (Parker, 2003) further identified seventy-six U.S. colleges and universities in thirty-two states, and three Canadian institutions in three provinces that offer master's degree programs with concentration in education of the gifted, including thirty-six U.S. and Canadian institutions that offer doctoral programs as well. Numerous materials have been published to assist teachers in the development and implementation of differentiated educational programs and services, and the quality of these services has improved markedly in many areas of the nation. Unfortunately, the field still has little (if any) empirical documentation regarding the impact of specific approaches and strategies on the degree to which our gifted students are realizing their potential for effective future citizenship—presumably the ultimate goal of all education efforts.

America's schools have typically been slow in infusing new technologies and approaches into their classrooms. For many years the only students who were given opportunities for learning and practicing higher-order thinking, problem solving, decision making, and technological skills were the academically gifted. Creativity was discouraged (indeed, often ridiculed or even punished) by "left-brained" teachers, and the use of rote learning far outweighed instruction in inquiry and other problem-solving modes. Activities designed to strengthen interpersonal communication skills were rare in the whole-class environment, and children's interests and individual needs were almost totally ignored in curriculum design. Gradually, bold educators began to break out of their "Second Wave" modes and explore "new" strategies—critical and creative thinking, scientific and creative problem solving, synectics, lateral thinking, simulation, group dynamics activities, and other approaches that had been used for decades in business and industry. This revolution is still under way today.

The field of gifted education has heavily influenced the introduction of new approaches into the general education classroom. At last, creativity, problem solving, decision making, interpersonal communication, and technology are being recognized as important for all students. Where does this progress leave us in gifted education?

Some time ago, when "school reform" was a relatively new concept, I attended a symposium on standards for gifted education. Prior to the group work sessions, we heard several presentations addressing the impact of educational reform on our field, as well as the potential impact of gifted education on general education. One of our visiting authorities began by complimenting the field of gifted education on the emphasis we placed on higher-order thinking, creativity, and other strategies not found in most classrooms, and by suggesting that *all* students should have opportunities to learn these skills. We were delighted to hear a professional of his stature expressing this view—until he followed it up by saying, "Then, when we have moved all of these strategies into the regular education program, we can get rid of these elitist gifted programs!" As many of us seethed, a well-known pioneer in our field arose and diplomatically but forcefully informed our guest of the realities on which he had not initially prepared.

It is high time for all children to enjoy the benefits that we have provided in gifted programs for so many years. Indeed, *all* children need to become creative, critical, and independent thinkers, to be able to communicate and work with others, to make logical decisions, and to solve problems. But once this happens, instead of getting rid of those "elitist gifted programs," we must begin to identify new approaches for challenging the unique abilities of gifted students that are frequently overlooked in the general education program, and for developing the special talents and contributions that they can offer to our society. To accomplish this task, we must first ask what we really want to accomplish through special programs for the gifted.

For many years I have contended that the major goal of gifted programs should be leadership development. While certainly I am not of the opinion that intellectual genius is prerequisite for effective leadership, I do firmly believe that our intellectually gifted citizens have the potential to become outstanding leaders—*if they are properly trained*. From past research and experience we know that above-average intelligence is essential for truly creative production to take place, and that knowledge is an essential condition for effective problem solving and decision making. It therefore seems evident that intellectually superior students who are provided with the necessary skills for leadership development have the greatest potential to provide intelligent and integrated leadership for our future. On the other hand, some of our most knowledgeable elected officials have been totally ineffectual because they lacked the skills required for effective leadership. Although it is widely acknowledged that Aristotle was amiss with his theory that leaders are born and not made, it is also apparent that leadership potential—like creative and intellectual potential—frequently fails to flourish if conscious efforts are not made to develop it. Finally, although we cannot realistically expect that all citizens who have leadership potential will in fact become recognized as active leaders in society or even in their own domains of expertise, it is logical to assume that persons who possess strong leadership skills are much more likely to become effective leaders or better followers in a diversity of problem-solving situations.

THE *LEADERSHIP TRAINING MODEL*: AN OVERVIEW

About twenty years ago my thoughts on leadership development for the gifted began to take shape. With the abundance of literature on the qualities of the effective leader, strategies for leadership development, tasks of the leader, and so on, that had emerged from business and industry, I was astonished to find that little had appeared in the educational literature about leadership development, and almost nothing was consciously being done to develop the leadership potential of our most capable students. After many months of agonizing, incubating, and experimenting with ways to visualize a new paradigm, I returned to the classic studies on leadership to determine the primary categories of leadership skills. Through numerous experiments with these concepts, I categorized the essential skills of leadership into four primary groups, which I have chosen to call *Cognition, Problem Solving, Interpersonal Communication*, and *Decision Making*. This conclusion resulted in the production of my *Leadership Training*

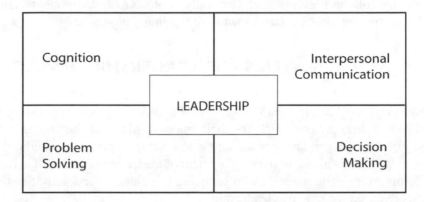

Cognition

    Exploration
    Specialization
    Investigative Skill Training
    Research

Interpersonal Communication

    Self-Realization
    Empathy
    Cooperation
    Conflict Resolution

Problem Solving

    Problem Perception and Definition
    Incubation
    Creative Thinking
    Analysis
    Evaluation
    Implementation

Decision Making

    Independence
    Self-Confidence
    Responsibility
    Task Commitment
    Moral Strength

The *Leadership Training Model.*
Illustration by Michael Pellegrin.

Model, first published in *G/C/T* (1983) and later presented as the fundamental theme for gifted program development in my 1989 text, *Instructional Strategies for Teaching the Gifted.*

The philosophy underlying the *Leadership Training Model (LTM)* maintains quite simply that (1) in order to ensure gifted and integrative leadership for the new millennium, leadership development should be a major goal (if not *the* major goal) of programs for gifted students; and (2) the development of leadership potential depends on the cultivation and application of those skills required for effective leadership. The model is designed in such a way as to incorporate those strategies that have been effective in the training of gifted students into a structure on which gifted programs may be based.

A close analysis of the *Leadership Training Model* reveals the deliberate presence of two familiar dichotomies. First, the structure of the model is purposefully analogous to the popular theory that the right and left hemispheres of the human brain house different but complementary mental functions. On the left side of the visual model are *Cognition* and *Problem Solving,* commonly considered to be left-brain functions; on the right are *Interpersonal Communication* and *Decision Making,* which relate more closely to the functions of the right brain. Perhaps a purist would find fault with this analogy, pointing out that creativity—a clearly right-brain function—is subsumed under *Problem Solving* on the left side of the model, and *Decision Making* (on the right side of the model) necessitates the use of critical thinking and logic, which are believed to be left-brain functions. However, much of the classic literature in cognitive psychology (notably the writings of John Dewey) clearly affirms that creativity is a cognitive process! Furthermore, a second purpose of the design (or one of the "methods in my madness") is to demonstrate the importance of interweaving the left and right hemisphere functions to achieve integrated thinking—and hence integrative leadership. The second dichotomy that is represented in this model is the concept of cognitive versus affective as defined by Bloom (1974). In similar fashion to the preceding analogy, *Cognition* and *Problem Solving* are chiefly cognitive components, whereas *Interpersonal Communication* and *Decision Making* are primarily affective. Once again, the goal of integration comes into play, since the integrative leader must be strong in both cognitive and affective skills in order to be effective in any leadership role.

The section that follows presents a detailed analysis of the *LTM* components, along with strategies and sample activities that might be used in a leadership training program.

STRATEGIES AND ACTIVITIES FOR LEADERSHIP DEVELOPMENT

Creative teachers who have received specialized training in the field of gifted education are cognizant of, and accomplished in the use of, a wide variety of strategies for providing individualized (or *qualitatively differentiated*) programming for their students. Many of the strategies that are typically practiced in the gifted classroom are appropriate for leadership training; we need only to reorient them into a new context with goals aimed at the development of leadership potential. This section will present steps in proceeding through the model, and a sampling of strategies and activities that can be used to develop the skills required for effective leadership.

Cognition

Cognition implies factual knowledge. More and more, today's educators are accentuating the need for advanced cognitive preparation in gifted education. President George W. Bush's *No Child Left Behind* legislation reinforced the emphasis on content knowledge. However, gifted students do not need more rote learning, nor more emphasis on the lower levels of Bloom's Taxonomy. What is needed is a swing toward training in cognitive *process* and greater emphasis on *higher-order thinking*. Also essential is the freedom to use one's own most efficient learning style and the ability to become a *producer* (not merely a *consumer*) of knowledge. With these goals in mind, the *Cognition* component of the *Leadership Training Model* comprises four stages: exploration, specialization, investigative skill training, and research. In addition to the development of research skills, the *Cognition* component of the model prescribes an emphasis on higher-order thinking, as well as studies designed to develop in our society's future leaders what Toffler (1974) calls a "future-focused role image" (pp. 19–32).

Developing Cognitive Skills through Research

Exploration is the first step in the drive for cognitive development. Comparable to Renzulli's Type One enrichment (1977, 1985, 1997), this stage simply exposes students to a wide variety of topics from which they might identify areas of particular interest or strength. While this step is merely what all good teachers do on a regular basis in their classrooms, it is nonetheless essential in the development of a strong content base.

Exploration can be accomplished through a number of simple strategies interspersed throughout any instructional unit. Notable among these are the use of community resources (field studies, guest speakers, mentors), classroom learning centers—especially the research-oriented *Interest Development Centers* as defined by Renzulli (1985, 1997), and effective use of modern technology (notably resources such as the Internet, HyperStudio/HyperCard, PowerPoint, and interactive video). Equally important is acknowledgment of, and programming for, the diverse learning styles of leadership trainees.

Specialization involves the narrowing process that results from exposure to a broad conceptual base. In this stage of the *Cognition* component, the student is encouraged to focus on a particular topic or problem for in-depth investigation. John Dewey is often credited with the observation that "A problem well-stated is half solved." The skill of problem definition, an extremely important stage of the creative problem-solving process, must be taught as a cognitive skill as well.

A major role of the teacher/facilitator in developing research skills is guidance in the narrowing of broad topics to specific questions for investigation. In the specialization stage, students should be provided with questions designed to assist in this narrowing process. Several steps might be taken in this effort:

1. Once a broad area of interest has been identified, the student reads material from several sources to gain an overview of the topic. At this point, subtopics are identified through brainstorming. An "Idea Tree" may provide assistance in this effort. For example, a student who is interested in science might produce the tree on the following page.

2. After further consideration of the various subtopics, the student narrows to one specific area—say, the raising of flowering plants. Additional reading on the subject, along with interviews of botanists and horticulturists, provides valuable information, including problems involved in the culture of flowering plants.

3. Finally, the student narrows the field to a specific research question—e.g., "How can I make a simple and inexpensive fertilizer that will increase the frequency and number of blooms on a begonia?"

Investigative Skill Training. Having identified the problem to be investigated, the student now must acquire the required skills of inquiry—the skills necessary for and appropriate to the topic or problem that the student wishes to investigate in depth. Of particular importance in this stage is the development of efficient skills of search. In the cited example, these skills might include training in the setting up of controlled experiments, the formulation of research hypotheses, identification of the specific nutrients that encourage plant growth and flowering (as well as common and inexpensive products that contain these ingredients), and so forth. It should be stressed that the teacher must impress upon the student (and guide the student in developing) the remaining steps of inquiry (the scientific method of problem solving)—gathering of data, note-taking and outlining skills, formulation of hypotheses, testing of hypotheses, observation and analysis of results, and formation of conclusions or generalizations. The teacher must also emphasize the importance of keeping meticulous and detailed logs or journals reporting on the daily processes followed and results observed. (An important measure of an experiment's value is its ability to be replicated.) Finally, attention must be given to the development of higher-order thinking skills and positive attitudes toward the future (treated later in this section), which are equally important in this process-oriented stage of the model. Once these skills have been acquired, the student is ready to begin the research.

Research. Following the narrowing down of a specific research question and the acquisition of the skills needed to begin a firsthand investigation, the student is ready to conduct the experiment and draw conclusions from its results. The Type Three product of Renzulli's *Enrichment Triad Model*—"a real product for a real audience" (1977, 1985, 1997)—is an excellent example of this type of application. With its completion, the final product of reality-based investigation and research achieves this goal of *LTM*, preparing the student for the lifelong continuous acquisition of new skills and information.

Thinking Skills

Some years ago, a study was undertaken at Harvard University to determine what the major goals of higher education should be. According to the findings of this study, the first requirement of an educated person should be to "think . . . clearly and effectively." This recommendation affirmed the early observations of John Dewey, who once commented that "learning is learning to think." If these claims

Idea Tree
Illustration by Michael Pellegrin.

are accurate, and if Einstein was correct that "imagination is more important than knowledge," our modern educational systems have been sadly remiss in the discharge of their duties. Even today, many "back-to-basics" advocates consider the inclusion of thinking skill instruction and practice to be a frill rather than a necessity.

The ability to think clearly—both creatively and critically—is essential to effective leadership. One of the most easily identifiable characteristics that distinguishes gifted youngsters from their less able peers is their intellectual thinking ability. Unfortunately, all too often thinking skills remain undeveloped, and the productive application of this innate potential fails to materialize. As Henry Ford so aptly phrased it, thinking [especially productive thinking] is hard work.

There are hundreds of companies that publish materials for teaching thinking skills in the elementary and secondary schools, and some of these publications are widely used in special programs for the gifted. Many writers have promoted the use of Bloom's *Taxonomy of Educational Objectives* to ensure an emphasis on "higher-order thinking," and the *Operations* (especially Convergent Production, Divergent Production, and Evaluation) of Guilford's *Structure of Intellect* model (1967) are frequently used to obtain a similar balance in gifted education.

Thinking skills constitute the foundation of all of the so-called "basics" of school. In the development of his unique model of the human intellect, Guilford theorized that each of the various components of intellect controls one or more human intellectual functions. Presenting educational applications of Guilford's model, Meeker (1969) contended that strengthening the components of intellect in which an individual lacked competence would in turn strengthen the ability to function effectively in the corresponding academic skills on which school learning is based. Similarly, it may be assumed that the development of efficient thinking skills will enable any individual to perform more effectively in the academic subject matter of which each of these skills forms a foundation.

In turn, the resulting skills are essential to effective leadership. The development of the basic thinking skills, then, might be seen as the cognitive backbone of a leadership training program for the gifted.

It is not possible to present here a meaningful treatise on the teaching of thinking skills as an important component of leadership training. However, several suggestions may be helpful to the teacher.

1. It is crucially important to recognize that critical and creative thinking do not conflict with one another. Indeed, both are essential to the problem-solving process.

2. Questions used in classroom discussion and assessment should include a large percentage of divergent items. While convergent questioning and discussion are necessary in the process of gaining and applying knowledge, teachers—especially those who work with highly able students—must go beyond this level of thinking in order to develop the creative abilities that will maximize leadership potential.

3. Although it was developed for other purposes, Bloom's *Taxonomy of Educational Objectives* (1974) has long provided a useful model for testing the levels of thinking challenged in instructional sequences. With the current emphasis on higher-order thinking, a comparative model (Kaplan, 1975) is useful in differentiating between thinking skills in gifted education and their use in general education.

As illustrated in the following graphics, the lower levels of Bloom's Taxonomy are stressed in the general education classroom in order to develop a firm base of content knowledge on which to build at the higher levels. Gifted students, on the other hand, need little emphasis on the knowledge and comprehension levels of thinking, which they have often mastered in the early years, and a greater emphasis on the higher levels of analysis, application, synthesis, and evaluation. By periodically classifying the activities used in class lessons, a teacher can easily determine whether or not higher-order thinking is being emphasized.

4. Students should be taught (and given opportunities) to distinguish between relevant and irrelevant facts, between fact and opinion, between fact and fiction. The ability to discern these differences can be developed through such activities as

   • studying newspaper articles and advertisements.

   • using editorials, television commentaries such as *60 Minutes,* and other current nonfiction reporting to provide practice.

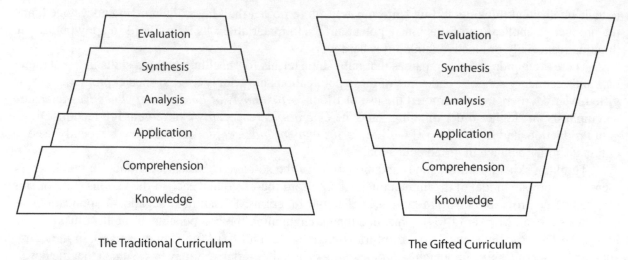

The Traditional Curriculum   The Gifted Curriculum

Bloom's Taxonomy and the Gifted
Adapted from: Kaplan, Sandra N. (1975). Providing programs for the gifted and talented:
A handbook. Reston, VA: The Council for Exceptional Children. Illustration by Michael Pellegrin.

- examining varied examples of propaganda (e.g., advertisements, political campaign speeches, and slogans).
- having students develop and write promotional material to help "sell" creative new products, run for imaginary or school office, and the like.
- using books such as *How to Lie with Statistics* (Huff, 1954) to show students how statistics are often used out of context to support a writer's position on an issue.

5. Logic—inductive and deductive thinking—is an essential tool for the development of effective decision-making skills, and therefore should be taught as a part of thinking skills instruction. Critical Thinking Press and others have published numerous volumes of activities designed to help students develop these skills. The cautious teacher, however, will ensure that these activities are integrated into meaningful contexts within planned lessons; gifted students do not need "busy work"!

6. Analogy provides a useful skill for many purposes. Research has documented that persons who are adept at solving analogy problems tend to perform well academically, especially in the area of vocabulary. Sternberg (1985) cited studies that produced high correlations between scores on the *Miller Analogies Test* and the vocabulary subtests of the major intelligence measures, as well as others that demonstrated that students who follow deliberate processes for solving analogies will achieve more efficiently in school than those who simply use free-association techniques for this type of problem solving. But, although the skill of solving analogy problems will be helpful to our gifted students in taking college entrance tests, the use of analogy within the context of daily lessons will be even more useful for life. How can the use of analogies be taught? The social studies teacher who compares apartheid in Africa to slavery in the early years of our nation, or cites the causes espoused in the American Revolution to help students understand current events in the Civil Rights Movement, is modeling the use of analogy. This skill is extremely helpful in assisting students to utilize prior knowledge in the acquisition of newer and more complex concepts.

7. In his model of the human intellect, Guilford (1967) included two operations that may be grouped under the heading of productive thinking: Convergent Production and Divergent

Production. *Convergent Production* is the type of thinking that is most commonly called for in the traditional school classroom. Contrary to popular misconception, it is not the simple regurgitation of facts presented and memorized; like Divergent Production, this skill requires the production of new information from given information. In Convergent Production, however, the emphasis is on the production of expected or appropriate responses. *Divergent Production,* on the other hand, stresses the variety and quality of the response (Meeker, 1969). The primary difference, as demonstrated in the terms themselves, is between focusing (or converging) and branching out (or diverging). Convergent Production is used in such activities as classification of insects using a taxonomic key, listing of synonyms for a given word, arranging historic events in sequence, or listing the leadership attributes displayed by a certain president. Divergent Production is commonly associated with (and related to) creativity, although the two concepts are not identical. Divergent Production is particularly important in gifted education because its open-ended nature encourages students to approach their potential more effectively than does Convergent Production. Divergent questions might ask students to think of other ways in which a character might be portrayed, to arrange a set of blocks in a variety of patterns, to brainstorm different uses for a cardboard tube, or to write a sequel to a famous story.

Future Studies

Alvin Toffler, author of *Future Shock, Third Wave,* and numerous other futuristic publications, once stated that we need to develop in our young people a "future-focused role image" (1974, pp. 19–32)—the ability to imagine themselves in a positive light as future adults. High-ability students who have the potential to become the leaders of tomorrow's society must have a positive image of their future selves. Without this optimism, they will be unable to lead effectively. Let us briefly reexamine the four components of the *Leadership Training Model* in light of their relevance for the futuristic curriculum.

Cognition. Appropriately differentiated programming for gifted students must be built on a firm base of knowledge in a variety of areas. However, the skills of information retrieval and the presence of a scientific attitude are necessary if the bits and pieces of knowledge learned through the general education program are to be made relevant. We must train our gifted students to be firsthand investigators in their areas of personal interest. This training must include the identification of real-life problems, the production (rather than simply the consumption) of knowledge, the development of usable products, and the communication of these products to audiences who have a need for and the will to use them. Paraphrasing Kauffman's observations about democracy (1976, p. 35),

> *Leadership* cannot possibly be effective if its citizens are educated to be clever robots. The way to educate children for *leadership* is to let them do it—that doesn't mean allowing them to practice empty forms, to make pretend decisions or to vote on trivia; it means that they participate in the real decisions that affect them. You learn *leadership* in school not by defining it or by simulating it but by doing it.

Problem Solving. The second component of the *Leadership Training Model, Problem Solving,* is perhaps the area of futuristics about which we hear the most in gifted education. The national Future Problem Solving Program, initiated at the University of Georgia in 1975 by Dr. E. Paul Torrance, was designed to foster creative, future-oriented thinking, to strengthen communication and group work skills, to train students in research techniques, and to develop critical and analytical thinking skills (Hoomes, 1984). This futuristic strategy is therefore an essential component of any effective leadership training program for gifted students.

Interpersonal Communication. Of the concepts repeated often in the futuristic literature, one of the most common is that future leaders must be adept in *Interpersonal Communication*. Without the ability to work well with and influence others, direct leadership cannot be effective. As suggested in the hierarchy of skills listed for this area of the *LTM,* the development of interpersonal communication skills must include attention to a realistic and healthy self-concept, concern for others, empathy, and cooperative working skills. All of these goals are stressed in the writings of futuristic educators. *Interpersonal Communication* skills are therefore of the greatest importance in the building of healthy future role images in our gifted future leaders.

Decision Making. This final component of the *LTM* is another area that is frequently stressed in the futuristic literature. In a very real sense, *Decision Making* is the ultimate goal of the future-oriented curriculum, as it is the skill that will in the final analysis show society the direction in which it must head for survival.

Many types of activities can be incorporated into either enrichment or content lessons to enhance students' understanding of futuristic concepts. The following suggestions are but a few examples; others are limited only by the teacher's creativity.

1. List future-oriented examples from past or present (e.g., soothsayers in Shakespeare's plays; astrologers who foresaw the coming of Jesus; utopian writings; new professions that are likely to arise from current technology; and so forth), and discuss their implications.

2. Explore the meanings and possible consequences of concepts such as *culture shock* and *future shock.*

3. Speculate about future modes of transportation or communication.

4. Forecast future changes that will be needed in your city or state.

5. Discuss the government's role in the future with respect to public health, education, international affairs, and other related issues.

6. Suggest possible inventions that might enhance the quality of life for our future citizens.

7. Debate the use of alternative sources of energy, the prohibition of handguns, or other current controversial issues whose consequences could affect the quality of the future.

8. Use a Futures Wheel to explore possible futures. Begin with a topic well known to all students (e.g., the invention of the automobile); brainstorm to form a web or wheel reflecting both positive and negative consequences of this event (see example that follows). Using the invention of the computer, conduct a similar session, projecting future uses and implications of modern technology.

9. Divide into groups of five to six students to write "Utopias." First, brainstorm characteristics of an ideal society, considering such factors as government, education, transportation, lifestyle, customs, dress, careers, leisure, religion, and so on. Design these various aspects of your ideal society. Find a creative way to present each Utopia to the class.

Problem Solving

If we believe that quality investigative research should involve the inquiry method, then the acquisition of problem-solving skills must be an integral part of the leadership training process. The *Leadership Training Model* proposes a six-step approach to creative problem solving: problem perception and definition, incubation, creative thinking, analysis, evaluation, and implementation.

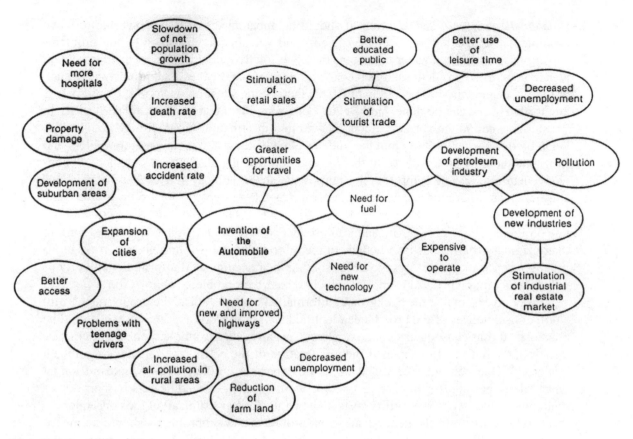

The Futures Wheel

Types of Problem Solving

It is interesting to note that, although there are many approaches to *Problem Solving,* most of these approaches have parallel steps. The primary difference between and among various approaches is their respective purposes.

Inquiry. Simply defined, inquiry is merely the use of research for the acquisition of information. The basic steps of the inquiry approach (or scientific method of problem solving) are: statement of a problem, gathering of data, formulation of one or more research hypotheses, experimentation or testing of hypotheses, analysis of results, and formation of conclusions or generalizations. The inquiry approach should be taught to all students beginning in the middle grades, and used regularly in the teaching of science and social studies.

Creative Problem Solving. Creative Problem Solving (CPS) is an approach that is designed and widely used to solve problems in business, industry, education, and personal life. To teach this process, have students identify problems that they would like to solve using the creative problem solving process. (Caution students in advance not to select for this purpose problems that are too personal to be shared in a group.) Work through the steps of this process as defined below. (Participation in the national Future Problem Solving Program is another excellent method of practicing the use of CPS, as the FPS process simply applies this process to problems of the future. Details on this national program may be found at http://www.fpsp.org.) The steps of Creative Problem Solving in the context of the *LTM* are as follows.

1. *Problem Perception and Definition.* It should be apparent that it is not possible to solve a problem that has not yet been perceived—and yet, this crucial stage of the problem-solving process is often either taken for granted or totally ignored. Once a general problem area (e.g., a broad problem such as global warming, or a highly personal problem area such as time management) has been identified, the facts of the situation must be explored before any further work can be done. In the classroom, a problem that does not relate directly to the students cannot be solved without background information. Thus, it may be useful to begin by discussing the facts that the students already know about the general problem and then send them out to search for further information. The popular "jigsaw" method of cooperative learning may be helpful for this purpose. With this strategy, the teacher first arranges students in small groups and assigns each group member a specific area to investigate. The students then regroup with others who are assigned to research the same area and collaborate on the development of a meaningful product. When the individual "experts" return to their original groups, they take with them the information gained through the investigative groups—hence the name "jigsaw." After sharing their accumulated information, all groups will have comparable backgrounds on which to base their problem solving efforts.

   Having assembled the background information on their topics, the groups next brainstorm consequences of the broad area identified for group work. At this stage it should be emphasized that consequences are not always negative. For example, consider a practice question, "What would happen if the temperature of the earth experienced a significant increase?" One consequence might be that campers in northern areas would no longer worry about getting frostbite, or that people would no longer need heaters in their homes (and thus would have lower utility costs in the winter). After listing all of the consequences that might result from the general situation, problems and subproblems should be identified for consideration. When all resulting problems have been listed, each group should review its list to determine the problems that are likely to be the most severe and in greatest need of solution. Here the teacher/moderator must emphasize the importance of specificity in the identification of the problem to be solved. In the example above, a specific problem might address the availability of food for human consumption. Rewording the subject into the form of a question that can then be answered through brainstorming, the group might restate the problem as, "How might we produce enough food for human consumption if the earth warms?" With the completion of this stage, the groups are ready to move on to the second step of the process.

2. *Incubation.* In his classic work *Applied Imagination* (1963), Alex Osborn, credited with the origin of the brainstorming and Creative Problem Solving processes as we know them today, recommended that all members of a brainstorming group be provided with a succinct statement of the problem to be addressed at least one day before the brainstorming session is to take place. Since the Creative Problem Solving process as defined by the *Leadership Training Model* begins with the perception and identification of a problem, incubation is included as the second step.

   Incubation is accomplished simply by getting away from the problem for a period of time. Once a specific problem has been identified and stated in a manner conducive to creative attack, the subject is ostensibly dropped until a predetermined future time at which it will be consciously reconsidered. During the incubation period, members of the problem-solving group should resist the temptation to address the problem consciously, devoting their attention to other topics as their "preconscious" minds continue to work toward a solution. After at least one day of rest from the identified problem, the groups will be ready for the next stage, creative thinking.

3. *Creative Thinking.* The third step in the Creative Problem Solving process is the point at which the brainstorming process is applied in its truest sense. At this stage, taking the problem identified in Step One, the group brainstorms alternative solutions to the problem. Crucial to the success of this stage is careful adherence to the four rules of brainstorming, originally recommended by Osborn (1963, p. 156):

- *Criticism is ruled out.* More often stated as "Defer judgment," this rule applies to positive as well as negative criticism. Even the use of positive reinforcement *during the brainstorming process* can discourage others from exercising their own creative potentials. ("That's a WONDERFUL idea, Maria!" may cause Martin to think, "If that's the kind of answer she wants, that's what I'll give her" or "I can't possibly be that creative, so I'll just be quiet!") This is not to say that encouragement and evaluation are unnecessary, but rather that the evaluative stage of the problem-solving process must be deferred until a later stage in order to foster creative thinking from all participants.

- *"Free-wheeling" is welcomed.* Wild, unconventional ideas are strongly encouraged; the more unusual ideas are offered, the better are the chances of obtaining truly creative solutions. The moderator should be aware that some types of questions evoke normally unacceptable responses from students, particularly those of preadolescent age groups. If for any reason the teacher is unable to gloss over such responses, a few basic rules such as "anything goes except sex and four-letter words" might control the problem before it occurs. (However, since this type of comment tends to restrict the creativity of the participants, teachers are encouraged to simply overlook the few such responses that occur.) "Free-wheeled" ideas are simply the result of flexible thinking.

- *Quantity is wanted.* The more ideas produced, the better are the chances of finding truly creative, innovative, and productive ideas. Quantity, of course, is simply the creative element of fluency.

- *Combination and improvement are sought.* Osborn suggests "hitchhiking" (sometimes called "piggybacking") on the ideas of others. As one member of the group shares an idea, related thoughts are spurred in the minds of other members (e.g., "Grow crops in the Superdome" might generate the idea "Build giant greenhouses"). The group must be encouraged to share these ideas, since they often become the most productive results of the brainstorming process.

Brainstorming is the skill that produces ideas in every stage of the Creative Problem Solving process. Ample time must be available for students to become proficient in this skill before moving on into the formal stages of problem solving. After providing periods of practice in the brainstorming process, the teacher should reiterate the rules and orient the group to the procedures to be followed. The importance of the physical arrangement of groups has been firmly established through research; whenever possible, members should be placed in one or more circles to permit the greatest possible degree of interaction. (If the group is fairly large, it is best to divide into groups of four to six members, to achieve the most efficient idea production.) To avoid overlooking good ideas of individual group members, the following procedures are recommended:

- To strengthen the concept of a group effort, a recorder should be selected for each group. Participants should be instructed to continue calling out ideas until they are recognized and written by the recorder. Other members can then "hitchhike" on the ideas recorded, producing a larger number of possible solutions.

- The ideal amount of time to allow for effective brainstorming is not agreed upon by all researchers. Parnes (1971) recommended that thirty to forty-five minutes be spent in brainstorming, to allow for delving deeply into the more creative ideas that may not come out in the opening minutes. Others suggest alternating between three-minute brainstorming sessions and five-minute incubation periods. Whatever time period is selected, it is wise to stop periodically to examine (and perhaps compare) the ideas of the various groups. Asking the groups to share at each break their two or three wildest/most creative ideas (emphasizing the need for flexibility)—as well as the number of ideas produced (fluency)—is an effective method of allowing incubation to take place while motivating creative production through friendly and nonthreatening competition. One final word: Although certainly a facilitator would not wish to cut off the brainstorming process when worthwhile production is taking place, Parnes recommends that the moderator estimate in advance the amount of time that will be needed. (Such an estimate can be made in advance on the basis of the length of time required to produce a good number of creative ideas in activities designed to teach and practice the brainstorming process.) If it appears that more time will be needed for effective idea production, he suggests that the problem be broken up into smaller, more specific problems that can be handled in a maximum of forty-five minutes each.

4. *Analysis.* When creative thinking has produced a number of alternative solutions to the identified problem, the contributions of the group must be analyzed and evaluated in order to arrive at the best solution. In this stage, each group recorder reviews the ideas that were produced during the brainstorming session. At the reading of each idea, the group simply voices its opinion, by voting yes or no, as to whether it might have merit as a solution or part of a solution. Through this method of elimination, the group narrows alternatives for serious consideration to approximately ten. At this point the evaluation stage begins.

5. *Evaluation.* The evaluation of the alternative solutions is accomplished through the following steps:

   a. Keeping in mind the nature of the identified problem, develop a list of four to six criteria that are appropriate for judging the proposed solutions. In our practice problem, these criteria might include such factors as cost, space needed, availability of the necessary technology, ethical considerations, time required for implementation, and so forth. In other cases, such as problems involving interpersonal relationships, these criteria may be irrelevant, and others that are more appropriate to the specific problem should be selected.

   b. Prepare a matrix, listing down the left side alternative solutions that were isolated in the Analysis stage. Across the top of the matrix, list the criteria on which these alternatives will be evaluated.

   c. Considering one criterion at a time, evaluate each of the alternative solutions. Again, let us consider our practice problem: "How might we produce enough food for human consumption if the earth warms?" Suppose the criteria were cost, technology, space, time, and ethics (as outlined earlier). Taking the first criterion, cost, each group would work down the column, rating each alternative solution as to cost. If there are ten possible solutions, the best one (i.e., the least expensive) would receive a score of 10, and the least acceptable (or most costly) would receive a 1. After scoring each alternative with respect to cost, proceed to technology, giving a 10 to the one for which we have the most accessible technology, and a 1 to perhaps one for which the technology is farthest in the future. Continue in this fashion until all alternatives have been rated with regard to all criteria, then add the scores across each row to arrive at the total rating for each solution. A quick glance at the last column should reveal the best solution (i.e., the one with the highest score) for the identified problem. There are, of course, times when this method does not yield a single "best" solution; for example, when a tie (or near tie) ensues. In such a case, the next step is to attempt to combine those alternatives that received the highest ratings. If this process does not produce a clearly superior solution, additional criteria might be added to help refine the decision, or the group may elect to use two or more sequential solutions, planning details for one solution at a time. With this final step, proceed to the last stage, Implementation.

6. *Implementation.* In an early discussion of the *Enrichment Triad Model,* Renzulli (1977) commented about the futility of having a basketball team practice regularly but never play a game. Similarly, practice in most skills with no "real-world" application is essentially a waste of time. So it is with the Creative Problem Solving process. All too often the process is taught in the classroom using practice problems—a worthy cause in the learning process, but a useless time-consumer if there is no transfer to the real world. The Creative Problem Solving process is much too valuable a tool to be practiced and then placed on the shelf with the classroom games. If not applied to real-life situations, Creative Problem Solving will become just another activity. In order to avoid this waste, the *Leadership Training Model* proposes that a plan of action be developed and implemented. In this stage, several steps must be followed:

a. *Troubleshooting.* Before developing the plan of action, the group should brainstorm to determine potential problems and ways in which implementation could be facilitated. Troubleshooting will enable participants to work on responses, change-agentry tactics, or other approaches that might make the solution more palatable to opposing parties. Also in this stage, the group should identify individuals or groups who might be involved or might aid in the implementation of the solution, locations where the solution might be piloted, and the like.

b. *Sequencing the Action.* Next, the group should brainstorm those procedures that must be followed in order to implement the solution (i.e., identify the short-term goals that will lead to the one long-range goal, the solution of the problem, and things that must be done in order to make the solution work). Finally, those steps that are decided upon must be sequenced in the proper order, thereby facilitating the action.

c. *Setting a Schedule.* The final step in implementation is the setting of a schedule—adding to the sequenced steps a set of specific dates and times when the various aspects of the action will be accomplished. With the actual implementation of each step, accompanied by interim (formative) evaluation, the Creative Problem Solving process is complete.

It should be noted that the terminology used in describing the Creative Problem Solving process varies widely in the numerous models found throughout the literature. The preceding adaptation was developed by the author for use specifically within the context of the *Leadership Training Model.*

The original approach to CPS was introduced by Alex Osborn in the early 1950s and later published in his classic work, *Applied Imagination* (1963). This approach was modified and published by Sidney Parnes in 1966, at which time it became known as the "Osborn-Parnes" method of Creative Problem Solving—a name still heard in many circles. After several decades of work and the publication of numerous versions of the CPS process, the system evolved into four components and eight stages. The latest approach, *CPS Version 6.1™* (Treffinger, Isaksen, & Dorval, 2000), guides the problem solver in using both creative and critical thinking to "understand challenges and opportunities, generate ideas, and develop effective plans for solving problems and managing change" (Center for Creative Learning, 2003). This version, illustrated by the graphic that follows, includes four main components (Understanding the Challenge, Generating Ideas, Preparing for Action, and Planning Your Approach), each specifying specific stages. The reader is encouraged to visit the Web site of the Center for Creative Learning (http://www.creativelearning.com) for more information on this process, which is commonly used in business, industry, and education, as well as a wealth of resources on the evolution and application of Creative Problem Solving.

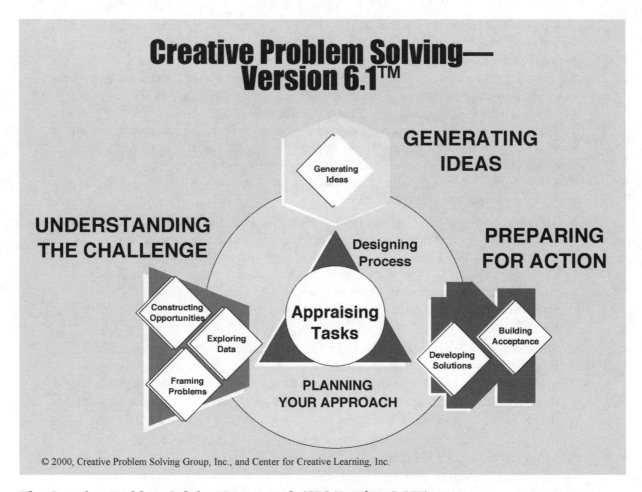

© 2000, Creative Problem Solving Group, Inc., and Center for Creative Learning, Inc.

The Creative Problem Solving Framework (CPS Version 6.1™)

©2003, Center for Creative Learning, Inc. and Creative Problem Solving Group, Inc.

Other Strategies for Developing Creativity

There are numerous other methods of fostering the creative potential of students who have the potential to become leaders of the future. These include the frequent use of brainstorming, guided imagery, synectics, lateral thinking, and many other methods that can be found in materials such as the *Gifted Treasury Series* (Teacher Ideas Press) and other classroom materials offered by a wide variety of publishers.

Interpersonal Communication

One of the primary characteristics of an effective leader is the ability to work with others. Often gifted students have difficulty identifying and interacting with their chronological age peers. If a major goal of gifted education is to train the gifted for future leadership roles, then it is essential that we train these students in the communication skills necessary for the development of effective interpersonal relationships.

Current literature in the area of leadership suggests that the development of effective interpersonal communication skills follows a continuum, beginning with self-awareness. The *Leadership Training Model* proposes the following steps in this continuum: self-realization, empathy, cooperation, and conflict resolution.

Components of Interpersonal Communication

Self-Realization. Maslow's (1959) widely accepted finding that creativity and self-actualization are closely related lends support to the cry for leaders who are mentally healthy, morally strong, and generally self-realized individuals. Research indicates that self-awareness and a healthy self-concept are prerequisite to self-realization or self-actualization. Many types of activities have been developed for this purpose. The use of dyad sharing techniques, the cautious and educated use of interest inventories and sociometric devices, and the application of group counseling techniques and other strategies are effective for developing self-awareness and self-concept. Above all, it is essential that the *LTM* facilitator be a humanistic educator—a teacher who demonstrates concern for students as individuals, values them as human beings, and displays empathic understanding (Rogers, 1967).

Empathy. When self-awareness has been built and the self-concept has been developed to a healthy and realistic level, the individual can begin to be sensitive to others in the group. Sensitivity to the needs of others, and the ability to listen and to recognize the value of other members' contributions to the group product, are essential elements in the building of group process skills. Until sensitivity, understanding, and empathy have developed, group cooperation skills will not be possible.

Cooperation. For a group leader to elicit cooperation from the members of a group, it is essential that basic communication skills be learned. The *Leadership Training Model* proposes the inclusion in the gifted curriculum of such basic communication experiences as public speaking, oral interpretation, parliamentary procedure, and debate. Once potential leaders have become skilled in these areas of communication, they are ready to begin the task of working with others. At this point the use of group dynamics activities such as Broken Squares (adopted from Johnson and Johnson, 1975), group projects, simulation, and the like, can help foster a spirit of group cooperation. The ability to work together in a cooperative effort is essential to the development of effective leadership. Also important in the development of group work skills is the teaching of social skills: basic courtesies, tact, and diplomacy. Finally, the ability to lead demands some understanding of human psychology, including techniques for persuasion and change agentry.

Conflict Resolution. Much has been written in recent years regarding the role of conflict resolution in leadership and interpersonal communication. Filley (1975) suggested several values of conflict in the group process situation:

1. The constructive use of conflict helps to diffuse or prevent more destructive conflicts.

2. Conflict stimulates the creative process through a need for new solutions.

3. The need for group cohesion and cooperation is stimulated by the effort to overcome the conflict.

The use of structured conflict and its resolution through problem solving can make an important contribution to the development of interpersonal communication skills and therefore is an essential component of any effective leadership training program.

Strategies for Developing Interpersonal Skills: Group Dynamics

The primary strategy that is used to develop interpersonal communication skills is commonly called group dynamics. Using this strategy, the teacher simply plans activities designed to provide practice in developing healthy self-concepts and the ability to work well with others. Numerous sources—e.g., Johnson & Johnson's Joining Together (1975)—are available to guide teachers in the training of this essential component of leadership development. A few examples are included herein:

1. Have each student create a "self-portrait." This might be a visual picture (painting, mural, collage, or three-dimensional model), a verbal picture (oral description, role-playing activity such as charades, or a poem), a psychomotor picture (a dance or a song), or any combination of these ideas. These "pictures" might be shared with others, although sharing should not be required in the early stages of self-awareness development.

2. Utilize boundary breakers as lesson openers. A boundary breaker is simply a question that is answered by all participants, preferably seated in a circle to allow free interaction. Boundary breakers should be nonthreatening to the psychological security of all group members. As the name implies, "anything goes" in the answering of the question. A few examples of boundary breakers that might encourage introspection are:

   • If you could be any person, living or dead, real or imaginary, for one week, who would you be?

   • If you could have any talent that you do not now have, what would it be?

   It should be noted that students who wish to share the reasons for their answers will voluntarily do so; adding "and why?" at the end of the boundary breaker tends to discourage open responses and therefore is discouraged.

3. Divide the class into circles of six to eight students, and introduce a topic with which all are familiar enough to contribute an opinion. At first, topics with no particular implications should be used (e.g., "Beauty is in the eye of the beholder"). As students become more closely acquainted, controversial issues (e.g., the use of nuclear power, the awarding of grades in the gifted classroom) could be introduced. Using this technique, the first person gives an opinion, and the next person affirms the first response, adding his or her own opinion. (For example, the second person might say, "What I hear you saying is . . . ; I agree with you that . . . ; however, I really feel that . . .") This process continues around the circle until each member of the group has had at least one opportunity to express an opinion. The value of this activity, generally accredited to the counseling techniques of Karkhuff, lies in the affirmation that each member receives, and the practice that it provides in attempting to relate to the views of others, as the discussion continues around the circle.

4. Provide small-group and whole-class group problem-solving activities designed to enhance group work skills. Numerous examples are available in the literature.

5. Whenever possible, utilize cooperative work groups within the gifted classroom to strengthen students' ability to develop a group product. The popular "jigsaw" method discussed earlier in this text is useful for this purpose.

Decision Making

The ability to make intelligent, rational, and responsible decisions is also an essential quality for effective leadership. Effective decision making requires self-confidence, independence of thought and action, task commitment, acceptance of responsibility, and moral strength. The *Leadership Training Model* proposes a series of planned experiences designed to develop these aspects of decision making. This component of *LTM* includes the development of realistic goals, the ability to organize and implement plans for meeting these goals, and the use of both formative and summative evaluation.

Components of Decision Making

Self-Confidence. Abraham Maslow's classic studies on the relationship between creativity and self-actualization provide strong support for the importance of self-realization, self-confidence, and a healthy self-concept in the development of a potential future leader. Although the preponderance of the literature on leadership style seems to confirm that the democratic style of leadership is most successful, some (perhaps bolder) writers have pointed out that leaders must have the ability to make authoritative decisions when the group product fails to achieve an effective solution. In order to develop this ability in participants, a leadership training program must provide opportunities for strengthening their self-concepts so that they can develop the self-confidence that allows leaders to make and adhere to good decisions.

Independence. A widely acknowledged characteristic of the creative person is the ability to utilize an internal locus of control, allowing the individual to think and make appropriate and productive decisions apart from the opinions of others. Independence must be developed through the provision of numerous opportunities for decision making that also, while protecting the psychological and physical safety of the individual, allow that individual to experience learning from trial and error.

Task Commitment. In a well-known model that defines his concept of giftedness, Renzulli (1978, 1986) groups task commitment with above-average intelligence and creativity, suggesting that it is the interaction of these three qualities that makes giftedness. While leaders must have the support of the group membership, their own commitment to the task at hand is essential if the group work product is to be successful. To foster task commitment in future leaders, teachers must build efficient work-study skills by beginning with tasks in which students are interested, helping them find ways to build interest in areas outside of their own interests, and gradually building the ability and motivation to commit time and effort to tasks that are high in group priority but may differ from the individual's own domain.

Responsibility. A fourth component of *Decision Making* is the desire and ability to assume responsibility for the tasks at hand. One of the most popular aspects of the gifted program is often the freedom to move about in the classroom, to work and talk with one's peers, and to select topics and methods of study. Throughout the school years teachers emphasize the blessings of living in a free country. And yet no hour goes by in this country without many instances of freedoms being taken away. We are not doing justice to our gifted students if we allow them to believe that our freedom is unconditional. Leaders must know that if they do not exercise their freedoms responsibly, those freedoms will be lost.

Moral Strength. The final element that is essential for effective *Decision Making,* and thus for effective leadership, is moral strength. There is little doubt that Adolf Hitler would be cited by most people as the consummate example of a charismatic and highly effective leader whose lack of moral fiber led to some of the most disastrous outcomes in the history of the world. According to John Gardner (1990), "Hitler had some qualities that would be counted as strengths in any leader, good or bad—his sheer force of personality, his extraordinary steadiness of purpose over the years, and his genius for organizing and mobilizing. But those strengths were turned to evil ends. His lust for power was an end in itself . . . he believed that the end justified the means. . . . This was no ordinary dictator; this was an evil genius. But the evil got out of hand. He was like a mad arsonist, starting with little fires, going on to great conflagrations until he himself was consumed in the firestorm he created" (pp. 69–70).

Much has been written in recent years about the school's role in the moral development of its students. Ironically, many of the most moral parents are the most oppositional with respect to the issue of values education in the schools. When I was writing my first book about ten years ago, I initially included a chapter entitled "Values Clarification." As with my other chapters, I gave the first draft to a friend to critique; however, in this case I selected a colleague who I knew was opposed to the inclusion of values clarification activities in the classroom. Certain that my approach would cause her to change her views, I was amazed when she returned the chapter with the comment that she still opposed values clarification. When I stressed that my concept of values clarification was to clarify the values the children brought from home, she asked, "What about the student who brings from home a belief system that says, 'Do unto them before they do unto you' or 'Take what you can get, because no one is going to give you anything'?" From that time on, I have made a practice of telling my students that values *education* (as opposed to values *clarification*) is not only our *right* but our *responsibility* as teachers.

Strategies for Developing Decision-Making Skills

Values Education. Essentially, there are two kinds of values. First, general or societal values—those values that most Americans hold dear. These are the values that are accepted by our democratic society and that all citizens are expected to uphold. They include respect for the rights and property of others, honesty, tolerance, and fairness, as well as obedience of the written law and concern for our earth's environment. Patriotism, courage, and a strong work ethic are important in the building of a healthy citizenry, and skills of diplomacy and courtesy are essential to effective interpersonal communication (and hence to effective leadership). Acceptance of those historic documents that form the cornerstone of our liberty—the Declaration of Independence, the Constitution, the Bill of Rights—is essential to the development of effective leadership for our future.

Personal values, on the other hand, are those moral guidelines that cause people to behave and live differently from one another—the choices that are not governed by law. These are decisions based on religious beliefs and customs, personal health and recreation, self-motivation, and the like, which affect only individuals and not those around them. The responsibility of the teacher is not to indoctrinate students with personal beliefs and values, but rather to encourage students to strengthen their own *positive* and *democratic* values systems—those governed by the values of society—so that they will live by them. Honesty is a value that is required by society; our laws prevent stealing and our schools prohibit cheating. When the teacher assigns an essay on honesty to a student caught cheating on a test, this teacher is helping the student to strengthen her democratic values to the extent that the student will live her life by them. The presumption that parents can provide the total moral educational needs of students is naive; the child who does not experience values education in all aspects of life will suffer.

Why, then, is moral (or values) education so important in the development of future leadership among our gifted students? First, by definition, gifted students possess above-average intellectual potential, giving them an earlier understanding of societal issues than their chronological age peers have. Like the Hitlers of history, without moral guidance in their early years they may lead others in the wrong direction. Second, we know that gifted persons reach higher levels of reasoning at earlier ages. The early acceptance of moral responsibility is therefore essential to guide these students properly.

Realistically, the concern about values education in the schools has not been raised because of teachers encouraging discussion in history class on the problems of apartheid or the moral aspects of the Civil War. Rather, it has come to the forefront as a result of the misguided use of "values clarification" activities out of the context of reality.

How, then, are we to train our future leaders in the skills that will enable them to make (and guide others in making) the right decisions for society? The *Leadership Training Model* proposes a series of planned experiences designed to develop self-confidence, independence, task commitment, responsibility, and moral strength—the prerequisites of good *Decision Making*. The purposes of training in this component of *LTM* include the development of realistic goals, the ability to organize and implement plans for meeting these goals, and both formative and summative evaluation. Classroom strategies that lend themselves particularly well to the development of *Decision Making* skills include values education and role playing.

As discussed earlier, it is the teacher's responsibility to reinforce democratic values in the daily affairs of the classroom. Democratic (or societal) values are taught when the teacher models consistency and fairness, when students elect class officers who undertake specific responsibilities, and when the class participates with the teacher in the setting (and sometimes in the enforcement) of classroom rules. Values education also takes place when the teacher incorporates value-laden topics into the context of instructional sequences (e.g., a discussion about slavery, a reenactment of the Boston Tea Party, and the like). In addition, periodic activities designed specifically to help students reflect on the necessity of adhering to traditional values can be of help. One such activity follows.

THE LAND OF THE SPHERES

Long ago, on the massive continent of Pangaea, there existed a nation which its inhabitants called Cartel. Now, the people of Cartel were of two tribes: the Cubes and the Spheres. Although all of these people had existed on Cartel for many centuries, neither tribe had been native to the area. Somehow over the years the Spheres had gained control, although the Cubes were in the majority. In order to preserve their way of life, the Spheres maintained strict command of the land. Only Spheres could hold office in government, and the Spheres dictated the curricula of the schools. Spheres lived in good homes, inherited all the finest quality of life, and always had the run of the land. Spheres became Spheres by birth; it was not possible for a Cube to graduate into Spheredom.

The Cubes, on the other hand, were slaves to the Spheres. Their children could attend school until the age of ten, but they were taught by Cubes (who were not well trained) in the ways required by the Spheres. Their villages were poor, with meager living quarters occupied by several families together. They ate only what they could produce, and they were allowed to leave their village walls only when employed by Spheres to do their menial jobs.

One day a bright new Cube was born. He spoke differently from his parents and peers. He talked of leadership, of better ways of life, of victory and command. They called him Lars, after the Etruscan Lord, because somehow they knew he would help them overcome their adversity. As Lars grew, the Spheres watched apprehensively. They saw in him a difference. And so, in a feigned effort to appease the misery of the Cubes, the Spheres voted to give Lars a post in the government. It was here that they made their fatal error.

The land of Cartel now has a new government. Run by Lars, it gives to the Cubes the rights of ownership, the best schools, and the finest ways of life. One cannot become a Cube, for Cubeship is hereditary. Although Cubes were for many years suppressed, they all are now educated. It is the Spheres who now are the slaves.

Answer the following questions, and discuss your answers.

1. Do you think Lars should have taken over the Spheres' cities and exiled them to the former villages of the Cubes?
2. Should Lars be merciful on the Spheres, recognizing that they were only trying to preserve their own way of life?
3. Should the younger Spheres be allowed to hold some important government positions?
4. Should the new generation of Spheres be punished for the years of pain that their ancestors inflicted on the older Cubes?
5. Would you have answered differently if the Cubes had been Black tribes in South Africa? If you had been born a Sphere? If Cubes were Puerto Ricans in New York City?

Simulation and Other Forms of Role-Playing. From the earliest years of our lives we have all learned to play other roles. The youngest preschool child is engaging in role-playing when talking with an imaginary friend, playing school, or dressing up in Mother's old high-heeled shoes and furs. Puppet shows and plays from classroom readers provide role-playing experiences for primary and middle-grade children, and secondary students are introduced through their language arts classes to drama of a more serious nature. When we dress like Julius Caesar, a circus clown, or an abstract quality for a masquerade party, we are role-playing. And very often, when we attempt to impress others with the selves we would like to be, we are role-playing in real life.

Role-playing activities comprise one of the most effective strategies available for the building of group process and decision-making skills in the gifted classroom. Most notable among these strategies are simulation and sociodrama. Applying Hyman's (1974) assertions about the values of role-playing to gifted education, the *Leadership Training Model* offers the following advantages of role-playing for the strengthening of decision-making skills:

1. People learn by doing. Role-playing enables students to continue in this method of learning by acting.

2. Students experience confrontation and conflict resolution through role-playing activities. Much has been written in recent years regarding the role of conflict resolution in leadership and interpersonal communication. The use of structured conflict and its resolution through problem solving can make an important contribution to the development of interpersonal communication skills, and thus is an essential component of any effective leadership training program.

3. Motivation for learning is fostered through active pupil participation and recognition of the relevance of learning for success. Role-playing provides these experiences.

4. Through role playing strategies, particularly simulation and sociodrama, students are given the opportunity to test (in a psychologically safe environment) the possible results of future actions. This advantage allows students to see that they can change and to some extent control their future destiny.

5. Role-playing activities provide immediate opportunities to apply what has been learned.

6. Simulation and sociodrama encourage the development of advanced thinking skills. Critical thinking is fostered through the analysis of alternative solutions; at the same time, the value of intuitive thinking is seen through confrontations that do not allow time for critical analysis. Decision-making skills are then strengthened in the process.

7. Finally, the (essential) provision of a debriefing session following the use of role-playing activities fosters the development of evaluation skills, which are a critical part of *Decision Making*.

The chapter that follows provides suggestions of ways in which the *Leadership Training Model* may be used as a foundation for developing a leadership training program. It should be noted that, although the chapter heading addresses the model's use in gifted education, it could easily be adapted for use in general education schools and programs as well.

ADDITIONAL RESOURCES

Flack, J. D. (1997). *From the land of enchantment: Creative teaching with fairy tales* (pp. 89–133). Englewood, CO: Teacher Ideas Press.

Flack, J. D. (1989). *Inventing, inventions, and inventors: A teaching resource book* (pp. 74–79). Englewood, CO: Teacher Ideas Press.

Flack, J. D. (1989). *Inventing, inventions, and inventors: A teaching resource book* (pp. 89–90). Englewood, CO: Teacher Ideas Press.

Flack, J. D. (1989). *Inventing, inventions, and inventors: A teaching resource book* (pp. 106–127). Englewood, CO: Teacher Ideas Press.

Flack, J. D. (1990). *Mystery and detection: Thinking and problem solving with the sleuths* (pp. 1–17). Englewood, CO: Teacher Ideas Press.

Flack, J. D. (1990). *Mystery and detection: Thinking and problem solving with the sleuths* (pp. 141–166). Englewood, CO: Teacher Ideas Press.

Flack, J. D. (1993). *Talent Ed: Strategies for developing the talent in every learner* (pp. 69, 72, 83–84). Englewood, CO: Teacher Ideas Press.

Flack, J. D. (1993). *Talent Ed: Strategies for developing the talent in every learner* (pp. 129–131). Englewood, CO: Teacher Ideas Press.

Flack, J. D. (1993). *Talent Ed: Strategies for developing the talent in every learner* (pp. 156–157). Englewood, CO: Teacher Ideas Press.

Haven, Kendall (2000). *Voices of the American Revolution: Stories of men, women, and children who forged our nation.* Englewood, CO: Teacher Ideas Press.

McElmeel, S. L. (2002). *Character education: A book guide for teachers, librarians, and parents.* Englewood, CO: Teacher Ideas Press.

Parker, J. P. (2003). NAGC 2003–2004 directory of graduate programs and services in gifted and talented education. Washington, DC: National Association for Gifted Children.

Polette, N. (2000). *Gifted books, gifted readers: Literature activities to excite young minds.* Englewood, CO: Teacher Ideas Press.

State of the States: Gifted and Talented Report 2001–2002. (in press). Washington, DC: Council of State Directors of Programs for the Gifted and National Association for Gifted Children.

Steiner, S. (2001). *Promoting a global community through multicultural children's literature.* Englewood, CO: Teacher Ideas Press.

Treffinger, D. J., Isaksen, S. G., & Dorval, K. B. (2003). *Creative Problem Solving (CPS Version 6.1™): A Contemporary Framework for managing change.* Sarasota, FL: Center for Creative Learning, Inc., http://www.creativelearning.com.

Chapter Three

Using the *Leadership Training Model* as a Foundation for Curriculum Planning

It is important to note that the four components of the *Leadership Training Model* are not hierarchical—that is, no one component should be viewed as more advanced than any other. Similarly, no sequence is implied in its presentation—all components should be used throughout the year. How, then, can the model be used most effectively as the basis for program development?

1. In order to share resources and expertise, it is important for teachers in a leadership training program to meet on a regular basis for curriculum development sessions. Ideally, this process should follow a specific sequence:

   a. Assemble all teachers in the program for a whole-faculty session.

   b. Brainstorm all academic topics and/or concepts that the students should be expected to master by the end of the program. After brainstorming, discuss each item in the brainstormed list until the group has reached agreement—though not necessarily consensus on all items. Next, considering each of the four *Leadership Training Model* components separately, follow a similar procedure to identify the cognitive and affective (or left-brain and right-brain) processes and skills that the students must master in order to become effective future leaders.

   c. Develop a scope-and-sequence plan that specifies the grade levels at which each topic or skill will be covered, and the subtopics or subskills to be covered each year. (This process may take many sessions, depending upon the structure of the program, the number of teachers and grade levels in the program, and so on.)

   d. Divide into role-alike groups (e.g., all primary reading teachers, all fourth- through sixth-grade enrichment teachers, all high school math teachers). Using the list developed in the previous step, make a collaborative plan within each group to ensure that all of the topics and skills relegated to a given level or area will be covered.

   e. Continuing in role-alike groups, consider one *LTM* component at a time, brainstorming *types* of activities that would fit into each topic or skill. Expand this list into specific activities, divided by grade level. When convenient and appropriate, consider collaborating on combined activities (e.g., field trips, speakers, and so on).

   f. With the assistance of a whole-group facilitator or coordinator, compare all plans to avoid duplication of activities from one grade or subject area to another.

   g. Continue to meet periodically in role-alike groups to add new activities, coordinating revised plans to ensure continuity and avoid duplication.

2. Prior to writing Individualized Education Plans (IEPs), administer appropriate instruments, such as the *Leadership Identification Scales* included at the end of this chapter, to determine each student's current level of performance in each of the four major areas of the model. Use this information, along with the graded scope-and-sequence plan, to set each student's goals, objectives, and evaluation procedures for the year.

3. When planning instructional sequences, classify individual activities according to their place in the *Leadership Training Model*, to ensure that all components are adequately covered.

4. Build into the year's plans a variety of activities designed to provide leadership experience. These activities could range from the setting of simple classroom rules and taking responsibility for school cleanup, at the lower grade levels, to campaigning for Student Council offices, performing organized community service, "interning" with area professionals, and the like, at the secondary level.

5. Teach the model to the students, helping them to understand the goals of the program and the leadership skills that it is designed to develop.

The pages that follow provide suggested charts and other management tools for using the *Leadership Training Model* as a program base. Examples are provided to serve as a stimulus for further ideas; however, the ways in which the model can be adapted (e.g., for different grade levels, within specific subject areas, and so on) are limited only by the imagination of the teacher.

Leadership Training Model
Activity Planning Charts

As demonstrated by the examples cited in the charts that follow, more than one *LTM* component can be covered in a single activity, integrative teaching is encouraged, and a variety of strategies may be used to accomplish almost any goal. Note that only a few subject areas and topics are included. The charts can and should be greatly expanded. Further examples of integration can be found throughout the units in Part Two.

Version One: Activities in *LTM* Components by Subject Area

Themes or Subject Areas	Leadership Training Model Components			
	Cognition	Problem Solving	Interpersonal Communication	Decision Making
Science		Investigate the effectiveness of a variety of conditions on the growth of plants.	Use small groups in a simulation designed to make students more aware of the importance of conservation.	
Social Studies	Use analogy to help students understand the problems experienced in different parts of the world with respect to human rights.		Form teams to investigate and debate societal issues.	Use activities such as "The Land of the Spheres" (Chapter 2) to help students examine their personal values and attitudes with respect to human rights.
Arts	Use drama to help students understand the implications of a piece of literature.	Teach art as a problem-solving process.		
Gender Bias in Literature	Have students analyze gender-related attitudes of various authors.	Use small-group Creative Problem Solving to help students identify ways in which, as society's future leaders, they might be able to influence the elimination of gender bias.		

Version Two: Activities using Leadership Strategies by Subject Area

LTM Component: *Cognition*

Instructional Strategies	Subject Areas			
	Language Arts	**Social Studies**	**Science**	**Mathematics**
Research				Research the lives and contributions of famous mathematicians.
Thinking Skills	Use critical thinking skills to analyze and compare short stories with different plots.			
Futuristics			Use a Futures Wheel (see Chapter 2) to speculate on inventions of the future that might improve life as we know it.	

LTM Component: *Problem Solving*

Instructional Strategies	Subject Areas			
	Language Arts	**Social Studies**	**Arts**	**Science**
Brainstorming	Brainstorm characteristics of various literary styles or genres.			
Creative Problem Solving		Use Creative Problem Solving to identify ways in which intercultural relationships might be improved within the school.	Explore visual art as a problem-solving method.	
Inquiry (Scientific Method of Problem Solving)				Investigate the relationships between various scientific principles.

LTM Component: *Interpersonal Communication*

Instructional Strategies	Subject Areas			
	Language Arts	**Social Studies**	**Science**	**Arts**
Group Dynamics	Use the *Junior Great Books* questioning method to discuss appropriate works of literature.		Conduct small-group and whole-class discussions on the value of "modern art" vs. the classical forms.	
Debate				Form teams and conduct debates on current controversial issues of science (depending on the grade level).
Cooperative Learning		Use the "jigsaw" method of cooperative learning to help students teach one another about a specific period of history, the lives of famous persons, etc.		

LTM Component: *Decision Making*

Instructional Strategies	Subject Areas			
	Language Arts	**Social Studies**	**Science**	**Arts**
Values Education	Explore racial, cultural, or gender bias in classic literary works.			
Simulation			Use the "NASA Moon Survival Task" simulation (Appendix I) to help students understand scientific principles involved in space travel.	
Other Role-Playing Strategies			Create a "human solar system" in the school yard to help young children understand the vastness of our universe.	

DECISION MAKING: AN EXERCISE IN BUILDING SELF-ESTEEM

Provide each student with a Leadership Development Chart (see next page). Give the following directions orally, allowing time for each step to be completed.

1. On separate lines in the first column of your chart, list your leadership abilities (including any that you do not feel you have utilized to their greatest potential).

2. In the second column, write all of the accomplishments you have made as a result of each ability you have listed.

3. In the third column, add other achievements that you would like to accomplish as a result of each of these abilities.

4. In the fourth column, list obstacles, characteristics, or behaviors that have blocked your accomplishment of the desired goals.

5. Select a partner with whom you would be comfortable sharing. Share your chart with your partner. Ask your partner to suggest other accomplishments you have made, as well as other abilities that they have observed in you, but that you have not listed. With your partner's help, fill in accomplishments you have made, other potential areas for growth, and strategies you might use to eliminate factors that have blocked their accomplishment in the past.

6. Change roles and assist your partner in a similar self-analysis.

7. In the last column, list short-term and long-term steps that might help you accomplish your leadership goals.

Leadership Development Chart

Student _____

Leadership ability*	Accomplishments	Potential accomplishments	Factors that may have blocked accomplishments	Strategies for eliminating these blocks	Action plan	
					Short-term	Long-term

*Examples: "People skills"; study skills; research skills; higher-order thinking; futuristic attitudes; creativity; problem-solving ability; strong values system.

AN EXERCISE ON LEADERSHIP STYLE: DISTRIBUTED FUNCTIONS OF LEADERSHIP

Advance Preparation: Prepare one Function Card set for each group. Each set should include six 3×5 cards, folded to prevent reading during distribution. Mark the cards as shown below:

Card 1: Leadership Role: Opinion Giver. (You have strong opinions about the discussion topic. You tend to be somewhat overbearing, expecting that others should agree with your perspective.)

Card 2: Leadership Role: Open. (You may choose your own position on the topic and the way in which you present it in the group. However, you have secretly learned that the group will be asked later to select a leader to conduct the group discussion. You badly want to be this leader, so you should conduct yourself in such a way as to influence the group to select you as their leader.)

Card 3: Leadership Role: Peacemaker. (You will do anything to help the process go smoothly and to prevent arguments from taking place. At any point in which agreement seems impossible, suggest a compromise position.)

Card 4: Leadership Role: Criticizer. (You have a generally negative attitude, never agreeing with anyone and making unkind and sometimes sarcastic, demeaning comments that make you unpopular with your peers. You have very strong opinions about the discussion topic.)

Card 5: Leadership Role: Agreer. (Although you have definite beliefs about the topic of discussion, you have a low self-concept and little confidence in your personal opinions. You feel a strong need for friends. To "buy" popularity, you find a way to agree with everything anyone says.)

Card 6: Leadership Role: Open. (You may choose your own position on the topic and the way in which you present it in the group. However, you have secretly learned that the group will be asked later to select a leader to conduct the group discussion. You badly want to be this leader, so you should conduct yourself in such a way as to influence the group to select you as their leader.)

Procedures:

1. Divide the class into groups of six, appointing an initial moderator for each group. The moderator's initial task is to begin the discussion, to observe the group interaction and make notes regarding the group process, and to bring the group to consensus after four minutes of discussion.

2. Give each group a set of Function Cards (one for each member of the group). Each group's task is to discuss a selected topic or premise.* In the discussion, each student is to play the role, and uphold the position, described on the card. Tell the class they will have five minutes in which to reach consensus on a group position. (Explain that, in this case, consensus implies that the group will have agreed on a position to report, although individual members may not agree with all aspects of the decision.)

3. After five minutes, stop the discussion and instruct each group to select a leader. (Allow a maximum of three minutes for the leadership selection process.) Instruct the group leaders to facilitate their groups' discussion of the process—primarily, the degree to which the various roles played by the group members influenced their decision.

4. Debrief with the full class:

    a. Ask the group leaders to share and compare what happened in their groups; and

    b. Discuss the implications of the exercise for effective group leadership.

*Suggested topics for students in gifted programs:

    a. "The most effective program for gifted adolescents is one in which the students remain together for the full day and are placed with non-gifted students only for lunch, recess, and physical education."

    b. "Students in gifted classes should not receive grades."

Note: If this activity is used in a traditional classroom (outside a gifted program), other topics should be chosen.

Variations: Other topics, roles, and positions may be substituted for those used in this exercise. (See list of Group Roles below.) Discussions could center around topics such as selecting a game, singer, book, slogan, color, logo, or movie, or perhaps reaching consensus on a noncontroversial/nonsignificant premise such as "The eyes are the windows to the soul" or "Beauty is only skin deep." While groupings of five to six participants may be ideal, groups may include up to eight persons; however, larger groups may become unwieldy. An alternate arrangement might be for one group of six to eight students (assigned different roles as in the groupings described above) to conduct a discussion in front of the remainder of the class, then for the class to make observations about the various roles represented and their influences on the outcome.

GROUP ROLES

Agitator	Eternal Optimist	Opinion Seeker
Agreer	Evaluator	Peacekeeper
Belittler	Expeditor	Pessimist
Clarifier	Facilitator	Recognition Seeker
Criticizer	Fence Sitter	Smart Alec
Cynic	Follower	Special-Interest Advocate
Deviant	Friend Seeker	Standard Setter
Disagreer	Hair Splitter	
Discussion Director	Idea Giver	Supporter
Distractor	Initiator	Synthesizer
Dominator	Interpreter	Task Commitment Fanatic
Doubting Thomas	Non-Participant	Universal Authority
Encourager	Opinion Giver	

ADDITIONAL RESOURCES

Haven, K. (1995). *Amazing American women: 40 fascinating 5-minute reads*. Englewood, CO: Teacher Ideas Press.

Haven, K. (2002). *Voices of the American Civil War: Stories of men, women, and children who lived through the war between the states*. Englewood, CO: Teacher Ideas Press.

Haven, K. (2000). *Voices of the American Revolution: Stories of men, women, and children who forged our nation*. Englewood, CO: Teacher Ideas Press.

Mendoza, P. M. (1999). *Extraordinary people in extraordinary times: Heroes, sheroes, and villains*. Englewood, CO: Teacher Ideas Press.

Chapter Four

Leadership Identification Scales

Student ———————————————————————————— Grade —————

Rate the student on each of the characteristics that follow, using the following scale:

1   Never (or seldom) displays this characteristic

2   At times displays this characteristic

3   Frequently displays this characteristic

4   Regularly displays this characteristic

Items listed under each of the four *LTM* components are based on research; however, because of the great variability among persons of high ability and leadership potential, no attempt has been made to standardize this instrument. The results may be used both to analyze strengths and weaknesses of individual (or groups of) students with respect to leadership potential and training needs, and to identify areas of need for curriculum planning in a leadership training program.

Leadership Characteristics	Rating			
	1	**2**	**3**	**4**
Cognition				
1 knows and uses efficient research skills				
2 displays good memory				
3 displays advanced vocabulary, richness of expression				
4 understands meanings and processes of leadership				
5 readily/rapidly masters and recalls factual information and new processes				
6 demonstrates a positive attitude toward the future				
7 can identify and adapt to various styles of leadership				
8 distinguishes fact from fiction or opinion				
9 is knowledgeable about many topics				
10 thinks independently				
11 expresses self well in writing, orally, and publicly				
Total number of checks in each column				
Number of checks × column value				
Cognition Subtotal				
Problem Solving				
12 is flexible and adaptable; readily accepts change				
13 is insightful and intuitive—reads between lines				
14 is often a nonconformist				
15 possesses effective organizational skills				
16 sets and adheres to deadlines				
17 draws conclusions/generalizations				
18 perceives needs and finds different ways to solve problems				
19 deals effectively with abstract ideas				

Leadership Characteristics	Rating			
	1	2	3	4
20 displays creative imagination, fantasy, and unusual ideas				
21 asks questions, demonstrates curiosity				
22 improvises with commonplace ideas and materials				
23 forecasts outcomes of certain actions				
24 alternates between logical and creative thinking and decision making as needed in problem solving				
25 possesses a good sense of humor				
26 determines appropriate criteria and methods for evaluating accomplishment of goals				
27 produces many ideas (fluency)				
28 is adept at identifying problems				
29 demonstrates task commitment				
30 thinks divergently				
31 tolerates ambiguity				
32 analyzes facts and assesses situations before making decisions				
33 solicits, accepts, and incorporates suggestions, ideas, advice, and constructive criticism from others				
34 is willing to take risks				
35 has and communicates vision				
36 keeps an open mind				
Total number of checks in each column				
Number of checks × column value				
Problem Solving Subtotal				
Interpersonal Communication				
37 discusses two sides of an argument without emotion				
38 delegates authority				

	Leadership Characteristics	Rating			
		1	2	3	4
39	credits and praises others for work well done				
40	displays enthusiasm for group activities				
41	cares about others, treats others fairly, tries to understand their feelings and needs				
42	acknowledges own mistakes, strengths, weaknesses				
43	works well with others				
44	inspires confidence				
45	offers constructive criticism in a kind manner				
46	displays good listening skills				
47	motivates others				
48	turns negative criticisms into positive goals				
49	displays good management skills				
50	guides group effectively in establishing a plan of action				
51	accepts viewpoints of others				
52	makes effort to remember names and faces; makes friends easily				
53	is self-aware, self-confident				
54	trusts and respects others, their rights, and their opinions; maintains trust within groups				
55	leads in group discussions and projects; likes to be in charge				
56	resolves group conflicts; acts as a peacemaker when necessary				
57	recognizes and values differences in individuals				
58	is patient with self and others				
59	is loyal to superiors and friends				
60	sets and prioritizes realistic goals for self and group				
61	keeps in mind the best interests of the group				

Leadership Characteristics		Rating			
		1	2	3	4
62	keeps group on task				
63	works well with many types of persons/personalities				
64	works effectively for compromise				
65	participates openly in group discussions				
66	communicates well with persons in authority as well as followers				
67	supports group decisions even if doesn't agree				
Total number of checks in each column					
Number of checks × column value					
Interpersonal Communication Subtotal					
Decision Making					
68	displays the courage of his/her convictions				
69	is usually satisfied with own decisions				
70	readily states and defends own viewpoints and choices				
71	is reliable, persistent, and responsible				
72	sets high personal standards and can stick to them even when others disagree				
73	insists on high standards for group activities				
74	has clear set of values that determine personal actions				
Total number of checks in each column					
Number of checks × column value					
Decision Making Subtotal					

Leadership Identification Scales
Form T

Score Sheet

Student _____ Grade _____

Cognition		
Cognition Subtotal (Ca)		
Total of scores for items #15, 17, and 23 (Cb)		
Subtotal (Cc = Ca + Cb)		
Cognition Total Score (Cc/14)		

Problem Solving		
Problem Solving Subtotal (Pa)		
Total of scores for items #8, 10, 50, and 56 (Pb)		
Subtotal (Pc = Pa + Pb)		
Problem Solving Total Score (Pc/29)		

Interpersonal Communication		
Interpersonal Communication Subtotal (Ia)		
Total of scores for items #11, 13, 25, 31, 33, 34, 35, 36, and 71 (Ib)		
Subtotal (Ic = Ia + Ib)		
Interpersonal Communication Total Score (Ic/40)		

Decision Making		
Decision Making Subtotal (Da)		
Total of scores for items #6, 10, 13, 14, 15, 17, 19, 23, 26, 29, 32, 35, 38, 48, 53, 54, 56, 59, and 60 (Db)		
Subtotal (Dc = Da + Db)		
Decision Making Total Score (Dc/26)		

ADDITIONAL RESOURCES

Bean, S. M., & Karnes, F. A. (2001). Developing the leadership potential of gifted students. In Karnes, F. A., & Bean, S. M. (Eds.), *Methods and materials for teaching the gifted* (pp. 559–586). Waco, TX: Prufrock Press.

Bennis, W. (1991). Learning some basic truisms about leadership. *National Forum, 71*(1), 12–15.

Bloom, B. S. (Ed.). (1974). *Taxonomy of educational objectives*. New York: McKay.

Davis, G. A., & Rimm, S. B. (1998). *Education of the gifted and talented* (4th ed.). Needham Heights, MA: Allyn & Bacon.

Gardner, H. (1995). *Leading minds: An anatomy of leadership*. New York: Basic Books.

Gardner, J. (1990). *On leadership*. New York: The Free Press.

Hyman, R. T. (1974). *Ways of teaching* (2d ed.). New York: J. B. Lippincott.

Johnson, D. W., & Johnson, F. P. (1975). *Joining together: Group theory and group skills*. Englewood Cliffs, NJ: Prentice-Hall.

Kaplan, S. N. (1974). *Providing programs for the gifted and talented: A handbook*. Ventura, CA: Office of the Ventura County Superintendent of Schools.

Karnes, F. A., & Bean, S. M. (1993). *Girls and young women leading the way: 20 true stories about leadership*. Minneapolis: Free Spirit Publishing, Inc.

Karnes, F. A., & Chauvin, J. C. (2000). The development of leadership and gifted youth. *Communicator, 31*(3), 31–32, 41–42.

Karnes, F. A., & Chauvin, J. C. (2000). Leadership and the gifted in the 21st century. *Tempo, 1*(1), 12–14.

Karnes, F. A., & Chauvin, J. C. (2000). *The Leadership Development Program*. Scottsdale, AZ: Gifted Psychology Press.

Karnes, F. A., & Chauvin, J. C. (2000). *Leadership Skills Inventory*. Scottsdale, AZ: Gifted Psychology Press.

Karnes, F. A., & Zimmerman, M. (2001). Employing visual learning to enhance the leadership of the gifted. *Gifted Child Today, 24*(1), 56–59.

Morse, S. W. (1991). Leadership for an uncertain century. *National Forum, 71*(1), 2–4.

Murray, J. (1997). *Thoughts on leadership, from Warren Bennis*. Retrieved March 5, 2002 from http://www.leader-values.com.

Parker, J. P. (1989). *Instructional strategies for teaching the gifted*. Boston: Allyn and Bacon.

Parker, J. P. (1983). The Leadership Training Model: Integrated curriculum for the gifted. *G/C/T, (September/October)*, 8–13.

Passow, A. H. (1977). Foreword to *A new generation of leadership: Education for the gifted in leadership*. Ventura, CA: Office of the Ventura County Superintendent of Schools.

Randall, C. (1964). *Making good in management*. Columbus, OH: McGraw-Hill.

Renzulli, J. S. (1977). *The Enrichment Triad Model: A guide for developing defensible programs for the gifted and talented*. Mansfield Center, CT: Creative Learning Press.

Renzulli, J. S. (1977). *The Enrichment Triad Model: Integrated curriculum for the gifted and talented*. Wethersfield, CT: Creative Learning Press.

Renzulli, J. S. (1986). The three ring conception of giftedness: A developmental model for creative productivity. In R. J. Sternberg & J. E. Davidson (Eds.), *Conceptions of giftedness* (pp. 53–92). New York: Cambridge University Press.

Renzulli, J. S. (1978). What makes giftedness? Reexamining a definition. *Phi Delta Kappan, 60*(5), 180–184.

Renzulli, J. S., & Reis, S. M. (1985). *The Schoolwide Enrichment Model: A comprehensive plan for educational excellence*. Mansfield Center, CT: Creative Learning Press.

Renzulli, J. S., & Reis, S. M. (1997). *The Schoolwide Enrichment Model: A how to guide for educational excellence*. Mansfield Center, CT: Creative Learning Press.

Toffler, A. (1971). *Future shock*. New York: Bantam Books.

Toffler, A. (1981). *The third wave*. New York: Bantam Books.

Toffler, A. (Ed). (1974). *Learning for tomorrow: The role of the future in education*. New York: Vintage Books.

Torrance, E. P. (1962). *Guiding creative talent*. Englewood Cliffs, NJ: Prentice-Hall.

Treffinger, D. J., Isaksen, S. G., & Dorval, K. B. (1994). *Creative problem solving: An introduction* (Rev. ed.). Sarasota, FL: Center for Creative Learning.

Yates, M. (2002). *Leadership truths . . . the 4 e's 2002 version*. Retrieved on March 5, 2002 from http://www.leader-values.com.

PART II

Academic Units

Introduction

Decision Making. This is quite possibly the most challenging of the four components of the *Leadership Training Model*. At least it seemed challenging as I was deciding which units to include in this book. I attempted to cover a wide variety of topics and a broad age range so that the units would appeal to many teachers and students.

The units range from sixth to twelfth grade. The subjects include *general leadership, nursery rhymes, fairy tales, and fables, science, advertising, the Depression era,* and *Shakespeare.*

Originally, the units were written to encompass anywhere from nine to thirteen days of a summer enrichment program, with each day's lesson lasting approximately two and a half hours. However, the units were restructured in this book for use by the classroom teacher. Each lesson plan includes an opening activity, activities designed to meet the unit's goals and objectives, and closing activities, which provide experiences in all four components of the *LTM*. I designed the units to be teacher-friendly and useable. As a former elementary school teacher, I recognize the difficulty of fitting something else into an already tight schedule. Therefore, the teacher should feel free to incorporate any or all of the activities described in each lesson. The lesson itself might be completed in one day, but could easily take several sessions to complete. Therefore, a single unit might be completed in a two-week period, but could be extended to encompass four to six weeks, depending on the needs of the teacher and students.

Each lesson includes numerous opportunities for the students to experience all four components of the *LTM*. Instructional strategies, skills, and primary *LTM* classifications are listed at the end of each lesson. Each unit includes all four components of the *LTM*, and each lesson is classified according to the component that is prevalent in that lesson. It should be noted that the four components are subject to the interpretation and application of the teachers. There is some overlap; some activities cover more than one component. According to the authors' interpretations, each unit includes at least two days of activity that are primarily centered around each of the four *LTM* components: *Cognition, Problem Solving, Interpersonal Communication,* and *Decision Making.*

Each unit also has a reference section so the teacher can access additional information if necessary. Some units include additional activities as well as Web sites that provide additional opportunities for the students. Each unit includes a graphic organizer, as well as a listing of the activities that highlight the four components of the *LTM*.

Each unit has a recommendation for appropriate grade level. However, many of the units can be adapted to suit older or younger students. Every unit incorporates higher-level thinking and both academic and creative endeavors. All units include opportunities for the students to explore a topic, create a product, and share that product with a real audience.

This section also includes a "template" with which you can create your own thematic units using the four components of the *Leadership Training Model*. Whatever the topic, you can be assured that you are using *LTM* components if you follow this template.

Finally, each unit is designed to provide enjoyable and challenging experiences while helping students develop their leadership skills, which is what this book is all about!

Lucy Gremillion Begnaud

Chapter Five

Dreams of Greatness

Originated by Suzanne Bourgeois, Adrienne L. Smith, and Carolyn Perry

Subject Area: Interdisciplinary
Grade Levels: Adaptable for All Grade Levels

OVERVIEW AND RATIONALE

Leadership skills can and should be taught. This unit was written to provide opportunities for students to think about leadership qualities that others possess, and to examine leadership qualities within themselves. The students will also be asked to plan for future goals through specific activities.

UNIT GOALS

- Identify leadership qualities of great people.
- Recognize leadership qualities in themselves.
- Develop leadership qualities such as self-confidence, organization, communication, and future-focused role images.

Dreams of Greatness *LTM* Activities

Cognition Activities:	*Interpersonal Communication* Activities:
<ul><li>Define leadership</li><li>Research on leadership</li><li>Venn diagrams</li></ul>	<ul><li>Create a "Figment" filmstrip</li><li>Discuss situational leadership</li><li>Describe "seeds of greatness"</li><li>Hope Floats</li></ul>
Leadership Training Model	
Problem Solving Activities:	*Decision Making* Activities:
<ul><li>Create a computer-generated description of selected leader</li><li>Determine elements of creative leadership</li><li>Creative writing activities</li></ul>	<ul><li>Complete a skit about selected person</li><li>Create a poem or recipe card on selected person</li><li>Analyze personal leadership characteristics</li><li>"I Have a Dream" list</li></ul>

LESSON 1

Leadership Defined/Leader Research

- Brainstorm characteristics of leadership: What determines if a person is a leader? Write all responses on a transparency.
- Brainstorm leaders students have heard or read about. Consider categories such as exploration, politics, literature, music, military, spirituality, sports, education, theater, business, art, and medicine. Post these ideas on a transparency for future reference. Create a random list, and then categorize if appropriate.
- East student selects one leader to research. Students will be given a copy of the Library Resource Map (see page 60). They can choose from a variety of resources preselected by the teacher, or go to the library to research the selected person. Provide details concerning how the information is to be gathered and documented, as well as suggestions for sources. For example, information could be kept on index cards, using at least three different sources, how to cite references, and so forth.
- Students should be told that this information will be utilized in a variety of activities such as a computer-generated presentation, a skit, or a variety of writing activities.

Strategies/Skills: Brainstorming, exploration, investigative skill training, research

Primary *LTM* component: *Cognition*

Additional Teacher Information:

If students have difficulty determining leaders, suggest some well-known persons in various fields: Christopher Columbus, Frederick Douglass, John F. Kennedy, Martin Luther King, Jr., Booker T. Washington, Elizabeth Dole, Frank Lloyd Wright, Jonas Salk, Dwight Eisenhower, John Dewey, Mother Teresa, Golda Meir, and others. Students should be encouraged to include local leaders, living persons, and women. Encourage students to look for factual data as well as interesting anecdotal information on the selected person.

LESSON 2

Poetry/Recipe

- Boundary Breaker: Ask each student to reveal to the class something original or unusual about his/her selected leader.
- Share a poem about Benjamin Franklin on an overhead projector. Explain to students that this is an adapted acrostic. If possible, have students modify this poem to create a standard acrostic poem. Compare the differences and the depth of information provided with each type (see examples of both standard and adapted acrostics and recipe cards at end of unit).
- Students will create one or more of the following types of creative writing about their leader:

Acrostic

Adapted acrostic

Recipe card

Instructions:

- To complete an acrostic, write the person's full name down the left side of the paper. Each letter should begin a phrase or sentence about the leader. The letters at the beginning of each line should be highlighted or decorated in some way so that the leader's identity is clearly visible.

- To complete an adapted acrostic, fold a sheet of paper in half lengthwise. Print the leader's name in all capital letters down the center fold. Write a poem about the leader's childhood, specific incidents, contributions to society . . . whatever appeals to the student. Each letter in the name must start a word, but need not be at the beginning of a line.

- To complete a recipe card, use a 5" × 8" index card and decorate it. Ingredients should include characteristics, contributions, and other information about the life of the selected leader.

Share poems in pairs, in small groups, or with the whole class.

Assemble poems in an anthology collection. Copies can be given to each student, and one copy should be placed in the class and school library.

Strategies/Skills: Boundary breaker, creative writing, self-confidence, self-expression

Primary *LTM* component: *Decision Making*

LESSON 3

Skit

Tell students to imagine they are meeting their leaders. Ask:

- What do you notice about the person?
- What is s/he wearing?
- What is the setting?
- How does the leader react to your presence?
- What questions would you like to ask the person?
- What answers do you anticipate?
- Write interview questions and anticipated answers on a sheet of paper.

Have students write skits about their leaders. They may choose any time in the leader's life. The skit may be for one person, or can include other classmates. Students should be encouraged to present information in a creative manner. For example, the person might be interviewed by a late-night host, or eulogized by a friend at a funeral, or talked about via E-mail, etc. Other students may be asked to perform in skits.

Specific information that must be revealed through the skit or by a narrator:

Leader's name and other biographical information.

Time period in which the leader lived.

Information concerning the person's leadership qualities.

Contributions for which the leader is best known.

Class time is used for writing, planning, rehearsing, presenting, and evaluating. Accumulation of props and costumes may be handled at school, or at home if needed. The presentation could take place on a different day than the writing.

Students present skits to classmates and/or to other classes, at parent–teacher meetings, and so forth.

Strategies/Skills: Guided imagery, creative writing, creative dramatics

Primary *LTM* component: *Decision Making, Interpersonal Communication*

LESSON 4

Computer-Generated Presentation

- Students should pretend to be the leaders they have chosen. Additional research might need to be completed with this question in mind: "What do you want the world to remember about your life?"

- Students will complete a presentation using PowerPoint or some other presentation software package that is available. Students could also use Internet sites to gather information, depending on the teacher's resources and the student's knowledge of computers.

- Teacher guides students through the elements of using PowerPoint. Elements to include in the technology presentation are:

  Graphics

  A photo of the leader

  Text fields with biographical information and leadership traits

  A question/answer section

  A well-designed, aesthetically pleasing, easy-to-read presentation

- Students present their computer-generated presentations to the class. Students might be asked to rate which leader they would like to learn more about after viewing the presentations.

Strategies/Skills: Role-playing, analysis, synthesis, originality, elaboration, listening skills, values

Primary *LTM* component: *Decision Making*

LESSON 5

Figment Filmstrip

- Prepare a reference center with biographical information about a number of leaders in a variety of fields. The information at this center could be student generated, computer-generated, teacher selected, or a combination of the above. Allow students to choose a leader to describe.

- After researching the major contributions of the selected leader, students will determine which information they wish to share with fellow classmates.

- Students will be asked to create a *figment filmstrip*. A figment filmstrip is an imaginary vision that the speaker creates for the listener. Students must be aware of the great need for visualization and descriptive details when creating this type of filmstrip. If time permits, the script should be written and practiced with a partner.

- Teacher demonstrates an example of a figment filmstrip. Project an empty image on a television screen. (Some television sets can be turned on to reveal a solid blue or green image.

If not, the television can simply be turned off to display a black screen.) Teacher begins to describe a particular leader, commenting with great detail so that the audience can begin to "see" that person on the TV.

- Students take turns describing the selected leader, adding details without including the name of the leader.

- Listeners will try to guess the name of the leader being described. If desired, points can be awarded for correct guesses.

Strategies/Skills: Creative thinking, analysis, visualization

Primary *LTM* component: *Interpersonal Communication*

LESSON 6

Situational Leadership

Students are asked to think of living persons they know who possess leadership characteristics. Have them write a short character sketch of those individuals and assign them pseudonyms.

- Form groups of four to six students. Have students share character sketches within the group. Present a fictional scenario (predetermined by the teacher), and let the group decide which character should be chosen as the leader of the others in the group. Students must be able to justify their selection (see examples at end of unit).

- The activity above should be repeated using different scenarios involving the school, community, local and/or state government, and so forth. A new leader should emerge with each change of scenario.

- Results from the above activity will be shared with the class. The real name of each leader will be identified. Discussion may follow, since many may know these everyday people. The idea is to allow students to realize that leaders are all around them.

Strategies/Skills: Analysis, synthesis, evaluation, communication, awareness of others

Primary *LTM* component: *Interpersonal Communication*

Additional Teacher Information

The teacher should have a representative list of school, local, and state leaders from which the students can choose, as well as a predetermined set of scenarios.

LESSON 7

Elements of Creative Leadership/Creative Writing

- After students have researched a number of leaders and their qualities and characteristics, review the list of leadership characteristics. Have each student pair up with another student in the class. Examine selected leaders and create a Venn diagram comparing and contrasting the characteristics of the selected leaders.

- Once the diagrams are completed, students will then pair with another group and create a new Venn diagram, citing the commonalities that were found in the previous diagrams. Students will compare and contrast these leaders and create a new diagram. Continue doing this several times, depending on the size of the class. What should emerge will be a set of ideals common to all of the groups, which the students can analyze and from which they can draw conclusions. Encourage students to elaborate on personality and leadership experience that helped shape the leader (see examples at end of unit).

- Students will then create a chart on transparency. Using Stryker's Morphological Analysis format (Shallcross, 1981), create four separate columns with the following headings: Character, Goals, Obstacles, and Conclusion. Students will brainstorm names or phrases to complete each portion of the chart (e.g., contributions listed under Character would include persons students are researching; Goals would include sample goals that leaders strive for; Obstacles would include stumbling blocks the leaders have faced or could face; and Conclusions would include the end result for the leader). Once the lists have been completed, number the items in each list. Students should randomly select one item from each category. This can be done by asking the students to roll dice to determine which item they choose from each category; "pick a number from one to . . . "; draw out of a hat; or any other method the teacher chooses. The students will then write a humorous story with the mixed-up combinations (e.g., Abraham Lincoln becomes the director of Microsoft. His obstacles include high school failure, which he overcame, and thus he became the manager of a huge corporation in New York City). Encourage creative thinking with unique and varied opportunities for the character in the story.
- You may wish to have students arrange themselves in teams of two or three, as this type of creativity usually multiplies when students get together and share ideas! Be creative!

Strategies/Skills: Creative analysis, creative writing, decision making, group problem solving

Primary *LTM* component: *Problem Solving*

LESSON 8

"I Have a Dream"

- Ask students to think about dreams for their own future. If desired, students can share these ideas with a partner, or the ideas can be shared with the class by writing them on the board.
- Have students read Martin Luther King's famous "I Have a Dream" speech (available at www.historychannel.com.) and list leadership qualities that the students think Dr. King might have possessed to make that speech. Select the two most important qualities necessary to persuade others to believe in and act upon a dream.
- Over several class periods, provide practice in written and oral communication. The goal is to create a personal "I Have a Dream" speech suitable for oral presentation to peers and parents. Several sources are listed at the end of this unit. Lessons in oral communication should focus on approach, stance, voice, clarity, body language, and facial gestures. The written portion should center on gathering ideas about personal dreams for the future, and compiling them in a sequential fashion that is clear to the listener.
- Have students, dressed in "Sunday best," present their speeches to peers and parents at a late morning or early afternoon luncheon.

Strategies/Skills: Brainstorming, imagery, analysis, communication, self-actualization

Primary *LTM* component: *Decision Making/Interpersonal Communication*

Additional Teacher Information

Current research notes the importance of goal setting and of writing down one's future goals. Many effective leaders exhibit this habit. Impress upon the students the importance of creating a "wish list" of things they would like to accomplish in their future. Create a list of ten items or more, complete with a checklist to record their actual accomplishments! Be sure to include both short-term and long-term goals.

LESSON 9

Hope Floats/Personal Leadership Qualities

- Make two lists on the board. The first list should consist of "quality" nouns (such as courage, laughter, strength, endurance, hope, love, anger, depression, and the like). The second list should include verbs (such as floats, endures, beckons, disappoints, destroys, encourages, accepts, wonders, believes, and so on). This activity was inspired by the title of a movie, *Hope Floats,* with Harry Connick, Jr. and Sandra Bullock. Students will be asked to choose one word from each column (or create a new word if they think of another response) and create phrases to describe themselves. Responses should be shared with a partner, including the reason that phrase was chosen. Each person will then introduce his/her partner to the class, describing the phrase chosen by the individual (see examples at end of unit).

- Have students think about their hero/heroine and justify their choice. Show students your "hero" sandwich! (This can be the real thing or a construction paper model.) This sandwich includes all the personal leadership qualities that you possess. Some examples include:

Chopped liver (shows **courage** because you have "guts")

Lettuce (shows that you **include everyone** . . . "let us")

Mustard (shows **perseverance** because it is a difficult stain to get rid of)

- After students make a list of personal leadership characteristics, they should find a sandwich food that might be a good analogy of that quality. Have students create their "hero" sandwich from colored construction paper or fabric scraps. (Each layer should look like the food.) At least four qualities between two slices of bread are required.

- Each "hero" is presented with an explanation of each layer as a choice for the leadership qualities selected. Sandwiches are then placed in a picnic basket for future examination.

- Each student is given a seed packet (prepared by the teacher in advance) with the words "SEEDS of GREATNESS" on it. Students are encouraged to plant their seeds in a large pot, or in a special garden, along with a copy of their "dream list" (from the previous lesson). If they would like, students can share with classmates what the seeds might represent in the way of personal growth and goals. As the plants grow, the students should be encouraged to grow in leadership qualities as their dreams are accomplished!

Strategies/Skills: Analysis, creative writing, self-discovery

Primary *LTM* component: *Decision Making*

LIBRARY RESOURCE MAP

Topic: Leadership Research

Person selected: _____

Find the following characteristics concerning the person you are researching:

leader's full name	dates of birth/death
place of birth and/or nationality	area(s) of leadership
leadership characteristics	failures (adult or childhood)
significant events from childhood	main contributions for which this leader is best known
significant events from adulthood	additional contributions

Peruse the Following Areas of the Library:

General Encyclopedias

Subject Encyclopedias

Examples:

> *Authors and Artists for Young Adults*
>
> *Something about the Author*
>
> *Current Biography*
>
> *McGraw-Hill Encyclopedia of World Biography*

Computer Software Programs, which include biographical information

Ready Reference

Nonfiction Shelves

Biography Section—This section is arranged in alphabetical order. The first three letters of the biographee's last name are listed on the binder. For example, a book about Abraham Lincoln would have the call number: **B**
                                                                                Lin

SAMPLE ADAPTED ACROSTICS

We know that **B**en Franklin was a leader in
almost **E**very area. He was a politician and
an inventor of a **N**ew musical instrument—the harmonica.

He **F**elt concern for people's safety and
knew the time was **R**ight for public fire departments. He
started lending libraries **A**nd insurance companies. Both journalistic and
creative writing came **N**aturally to him. He was

well-**K**nown as an ambassador to France. His contribution to
the Declaration of Independence is **L**egendary. He was also active
In the Constitutional Convention.
Science, philosophy—there was **N**o area in which he wasn't a leader.

Amelia Earhart is one
of the **M**ost famous female
pilots **E**ver to live.
She **L**aughed in the face of danger.
If she ever had any chance to set a record,
She **A**lways did.

In the **E**arly 1900s, she became
The first woman to cross the **A**tlantic Ocean alone.
She set a number of other **R**ecords in speed and altitude.
But, she is known most for **H**er last flight on July 2, 1937.
Her career came to an **E**nd when
Her **A**irplane disappeared on an attempt to fly
Around the world. Any **R**emaining parts of the plane
Were never recovered. **T**he mystery has never been solved.

John Fitzgerald Kennedy
Had **O**penness to new ideas. In
Brookline, MA, **H**e was born on May 29, 1917.
He wrote for the college **N**ewspaper. He wrote about

Sailing, swimming, **F**ootball, and other sports. He was a

very **K**ind and gentle man. He was the youngest man
ever **E**lected to be president at 43 years.
Before that he served in the US **N**avy and saved a man's life.
John Kennedy's **N**ickname was "Jack." Everyone thought he had
A lot of energy and **E**nthusiasm. The 35th president of the United States was
Assassinated in **D**allas, Texas on November 22, 1963. He was
Famous for his **Y**outh until his untimely death.

Thomas Edison was a very
Interesting boy. When **H**e was 6 years old, he made a
Friend take a triple dose **O**f laxative to fill him
With gas so he could **M**omentarily fly. Unfortunately,
it didn't work **A**nd the boy lay sick on the
ground. Another **S**enseless experiment of his was

when he sat on **E**ggs to make them hatch.
Once again it **D**idn't work. But he didn't give up.
Thomas was an **I**nventor at a very young age.
Although he did some **S**illy things, soon he was to become
world famous, because **O**f his invention of the phonograph.
He believed in himself and **N**ever gave up.

She taught at St. **M**ary's High School in Calcutta, India.
When she was **O**lder she had a call to help
Teach the poor. She accepted
And all through her life she **H**elped the sick and homeless.
She thoroughly **E**njoyed what she did.
She **R**eceived the Nobel Peace Prize

In 1979. She used **T**he $25,000 to build the leper
Colony in West Bengal. **E**ventually she founded the order
Of the Missionaries of Charity. They **R**eceived the official status of
The Church from the Pope. **E**veryone had heard of Mother Teresa by this time.
She **S**uffered heart problems, which
Forced her to pass on **A**ll of her work to the Sisters of Charity.

SAMPLE ACROSTIC

Born in Boston, Massachusetts—1706
Editor and publisher of Poor Richard's Almanac
Noted American Statesman; signed the Declaration of Independence

Founded academy now known as University of Pennsylvania
Remembered as a publisher, printer, philosopher
Ambassador to France
Negotiated peace with Great Britain—1781–1783
Knowledgeable in establishing public libraries
Lighting of city streets
Inventor of harmonica, bifocals, stove
Not "shocked" by kite/electricity experiment

RECIPE FOR LEADERSHIP—BEN FRANKLIN

2 pounds **patriotism**
3 cups **courage**
5 liters **intelligence**
10 ounces **curiosity**
1 ounce **luck**
6 cups **philosophy**

SAMPLE SKETCH

The sketch should include the following information:

Pseudonym _____

Educational Background _____

Family Life _____

Religion _____

Occupation _____

Hobbies, Interests _____

Other Information _____

SAMPLE SCENARIOS

For each of the following scenarios, determine which leader you would choose to help remedy the situation:

- Your mom locked her keys in the car . . .
- A bully is picking on your friends . . .
- You have difficulty taking math tests . . .
- Someone you know has been (falsely) accused of cheating . . .
- (Create additional scenarios with the help of the students)

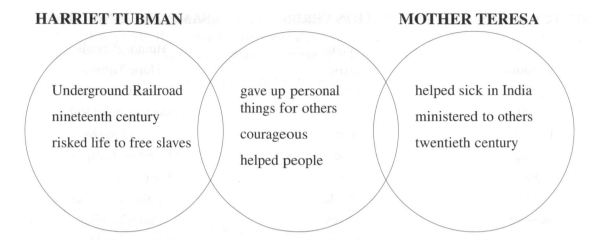

HARRIET TUBMAN

Underground Railroad

nineteenth century

risked life to free slaves

gave up personal things for others

courageous

helped people

MOTHER TERESA

helped sick in India

ministered to others

twentieth century

Students would then look at the center circle for both diagrams and see if they could come to some conclusions about common characteristics that leaders possess.

Chapter Six

Nursery "Mines," "Me"sop Fables, and "For Real" Tales

Originated by Cheryl Friberg

Subject Area: Language Arts

Grade Levels: Adaptable for All Grade Levels

OVERVIEW AND RATIONALE

The purpose of these lessons is to delve into the origins of Mother Goose, Aesop's Fables, and fairy tales while providing authentic teaching strategies for literary development. It is important for teachers of older students to know that nursery rhymes, fables, and fairy tales were originally written by adults for adults. They were reflections of the political perils of the times. This information, provided by the teacher, is meant to entice students to initiate their own research into the original purposes of these stories.

In this unit, students at all levels incorporate familiar stories and rhymes into flexible, creative writings. They will use their own autobiographical experiences to write about their personal feelings and ideas. The poems and stories become their own as they insert individual personalities into their writings to make them "mine" and about "me." The students use their own life experiences and a variety of thinking, problem solving, communication, and decision making methods to create new rhymes based on the traditional versions. Students are free to utilize creativity as they incorporate a bit of themselves into nursery rhymes and fables. It is necessary that the teacher maintains the nature and flow of these activities by creating a safe environment where students are able to take risks and set boundaries for the type of creativity that is expected, i.e., "G" rated or "No X-Rated" rhymes and fables.

UNIT GOALS

- Manipulate ideas, words, and sounds in Mother Goose rhymes to facilitate their rhyming ability and word attack skills.
- Become more fluent in reading, creative in imagination, and flexible in thinking.
- Create unique fables using problem solving strategies, originality, and research based upon personal experiences and lessons that life has taught while studying democratic values in our society.
- Be introduced to and/or research the historical aspects of Mother Goose rhymes and Aesop's Fables in order to better appreciate and understand the significance of these genres in literature.

Nursery "Mines," "Me"Sop Fables, and "For Real" Tales
LTM Activities

Cognition Activities:	*Interpersonal Communication* Activities:
• Research of nursery rhymes, fables, and fairy tales • Character-istics • "For Real" tales • Happily-EVEN-after	• Creative Dramatics activities • Life, so far • Author's party for guests • Character-US-sticks/ Character-THEM-sticks
Leadership Training Model	
Problem Solving Activities:	*Decision Making* Activities:
• The Ant and the Grasshopper • Matrix rhyme	• Twinkle, Twinkle, Little Star • Curds and What? • Magazine rhymes

LESSON 1

Eensy Weensy Spider

- Students introduce themselves using an adjective with the same beginning letter sound as their first name. Teacher will create a name tag for each of their new titles (ex: Joking Jeanette, Bold Billy, Laughing Lucy, Brilliant Barbara). (Teacher may need to remind the students that the adjectives need to be "G" rated; no "X"-rated adjectives.)

- Teacher will introduce the "Rhyme Ball": a standard soccer ball on which the teacher has marked the white sections with the names of familiar nursery rhymes. Students sit in a circle and toss the ball to one another. As a student catches it, the rhyme that is closest to his thumb has to be recited. Intermediate and secondary teachers will challenge their students to recall nursery rhymes from their childhood as a class, or pull rhyme titles out of a hat, basket, or decorated box for the class to recite.

- Students will be assigned to read nursery rhymes to a younger sibling or neighbor. Teacher gives a brief history of some of the rhymes mentioned, challenging students to research further with their parents and on their own. (See history at end of unit.)

- Ask students to recall the "Eensy Weensy Spider," acting out the finger play. Secure a copy of the book *The Eensy Weensy Spider,* adapted by Mary Ann Hoberman, illustrated by Nadine Bernard Westcott.

- Discuss the story. Ask students to compare it to the traditional nursery rhyme. How was this story different? (Elaboration.) In small groups, students will create an original elaboration of the "Eensy Weensy Spider" poem. (See examples at end of unit.) If time permits, students can experiment by creating various other rhyme elaborations by changing rhymes such as "Jack and Jill" or "Baa Baa Black Sheep."

- Recite together the nursery rhyme "Jack and Jill." Ask the following questions (reminding students of the "G" rating):

What are some other reasons Jack and Jill could have gone up the hill? Where else could they have gone? What if it were Jill who had fallen? Who else could have gone up the hill? Perhaps another nursery character? What other reason might they have had for going up the hill?

Share ideas (divergent), then narrow down the possibilities (convergent). In groups, create new rhymes with the new scenarios, maintaining the rhythm pattern. Share with others in a creative manner, such as singing, acting it out, using hand motions, and so on.

- Students could make their own books with construction paper covers. The children can decorate the book cover. One side of the book is for the rhymes, then flip the book upside down and turn it over for the fables portion of the book. The result: A unique flipbook with both types of writings!

- Summarize the day's activities. Challenge students to 1) create other rhymes at home, 2) volunteer to read nursery rhymes to younger children or, 3) research the history of other rhymes.

Strategies/Skills: Shared research, fluency, flexibility, originality, creative dramatics

Primary *LTM* component: *Cognition, Interpersonal Communication*

LESSON 2

Peter Piper *Alliteration and Alteration of Other Nursery Rhymes*

Today students will brainstorm letter words and create tongue twisters.

- Have students recall their alliteration names from Lesson 1, then recite the tongue twister "Peter Piper picked a peck of pickled peppers" first slowly, then increasing the pace. Students try to recite it. They will then try to create an alliteration rhyme using their name from Lesson 1. (See example at end of unit.)

- Ask students what they like to do when they are alone. Read the nursery rhyme "Little Jumping Joan" (see poem at end of unit). Ask them to think about how they can make a rhyme using their alliteration name and incorporate it into what they like to do when alone. Share in pairs, and then with the whole group.

- Teacher reads "Twinkle, Twinkle, Little Star" and relates this rhyme to the idea that all of them are stars with their own unique talents. Students determine two or three talents or traits that make them special. Students will find a quiet spot in the room to think, incubate, and reflect upon creating a rhyme about themselves that begins with "Twinkle, Twinkle, Little Star. How I wonder what you are?" while maintaining the original rhythm of "Twinkle, Twinkle, Little Star." (See examples at end of unit.)

- As closure for the day, students are asked to write a trivia question that pertains to nursery rhymes. Students are also encouraged to research on the computer or texts at home to create other trivia questions that will challenge their classmates. These will be incorporated into a trivia game at the end of teaching this unit (see listing of sample trivia questions at end of unit).

Surprisingly, although these seem to be too elementary, older students may not have had prior knowledge or they may have forgotten them! This should be a fun and interesting unit, as students learn to enjoy playing with words!

Strategies/Skills: Collaboration, problem solving, creativity, risk taking

Primary *LTM* component: *Decision Making*

LESSON 3

Curds and What? And What an Example!

- Recite the rhyme "Little Miss Muffet." Ask: What are "curds and whey?" It might be a good idea to ask this question a day ahead of this lesson so the students can complete research on the Internet or some other source at home. Then you can begin class with an open discussion of what was discovered from their research.

- Teacher will display a carton of cottage cheese, explaining what *curds and whey* are in the cheese. Students will be asked to take a risk by tasting the cottage cheese plain. Then the teacher will add sugar and cinnamon, or fruit, to the cottage cheese and ask students to taste again. (Be sure to check child's records for food allergies before allowing them to taste.)

- Using flexibility of selecting other creatures and fluency of ideas, the students will create a rhyme based upon "Little Miss Muffet."

- Read the rhyme "The Old Woman in the Shoe." Discuss the example the Old Woman is portraying about how to treat children. Guide the students into a brainstorm of different strategies for the Old Woman to use while putting her children to bed. Read "Old King Cole." Discuss the habit of smoking. What are some alternatives to smoking? Flexibility is encouraged, and students should experience joy while imagining a wide array of scenarios. Students will create their own rhyme of "Old Woman in the Shoe" or "Old King Cole," using better examples than what the original rhymes suggest. Write their unique rhyme(s) in their personal books and illustrate them.

- As a culminating activity, the students will share the new rhyme that they wrote.

Strategies/Skills: Incubation, reflection, creativity, risk taking

Primary *LTM* component: *Decision Making*

LESSON 4

Prop and Magazine Rhymes

- Selecting from a tray with various everyday objects (a pencil, a notebook, a baseball glove, a spoon, and the like), students will use the object as a prop for a nursery rhyme or nursery "mine." (e.g., *Mary had a little book/Its pages were fun to read/And everywhere that Mary went/Her book she knew she'd need!*)

- Display an assortment of magazines for the students to look through. Have students create their own magazine nursery "mines" by choosing one or more pictures and creating a rhyme, possibly piggybacking off Mother Goose rhymes. These rhymes may be written in the students' own handwriting, or taken from words and letters cut out of magazines, producing a collage effect (e.g., cartoon picture of boy standing in front of clock with baseball cap on head, inner tube around waist, violin in right hand, bag lunch in left hand, flippers on feet, and baseball on the ground).

- Before writing the magazine rhyme, students will be given an opportunity to elaborate on the magazine picture in large or small groups, if desired. Encourage them to look for interesting borders or frames within the magazine to elaborate their writings.

- Place a 6 × 6 grid on the board or on the overhead projector. Students are asked to name six nursery rhymes, which teacher records across the top six sections. Again, students suggest six different nursery rhymes and the teacher records these along the side sections. A student is called up and asked to place an "x" anywhere in the matrix. This will force the selection between words and images from two different rhymes. Students will create a new rhyme using words and images from both rhymes. Note: This could be a whole class, a small group, or an individual activity. (See examples at end of unit.)

- Using the rhyme ball (described in Lesson 1) or pulling rhymes out of a hat, encourage students to apply the strategies learned in this unit (changing one thing about the rhyme, force fitting two rhymes, using magazine pictures, creating an autobiographical rhyme). Change part of the rhyme to create an impromptu nursery rhyme with the help of the group.

- Watch the musical video *The Real Story of Itsy Bitsy Spider* (see reference at end of unit) as a way of bringing full circle the unit's activities by allowing the students to see creative variances. (This is optimal for older students.) Or search the library shelves for alternate versions of other Mother Goose stories.

- As a culminating activity, the students will use their new knowledge of rhymes from class exercises and research. Play a game of "Stump the Teacher" or any other trivia type game adapted for class use (e.g., How many bags of wool were given out in "Baa Baa Black Sheep"? Where's the little boy who lost the sheep?) Note: Older students will create a more challenging trivia by including research findings (e.g., The idea of forced, excessive taxation is in what rhyme?)

Strategies/Skills: Forced choices, creativity, fluency

Primary *LTM* component: *Decision Making, Interpersonal Communication*

LESSON 5

"ME"sop Character-istic

- Students will be given an opportunity to delve into the world of fables. Ask students how they decide what is right or wrong. How do they come to these decisions? Do they receive guidance from others concerning what is right or wrong?

- Question students as to previous knowledge concerning Aesop's Fables. Ask students if they have ever heard the story of "The Crow and the Pitcher," or "The Hare and the Tortoise," or "The City Mouse and the Country Mouse." Teacher will share information on the history of Aesop and his fables (see history at end of unit). Engage the students in searching for differences between fables and nursery rhymes.

- Read "The Fox and the Woodsman," or some other appropriate Aesop Fable. Students should determine as a group what the MORAL is. (In this fable, the moral is *Actions speak louder than words,* or *You should not do one thing and say another.*) Continue a discussion concerning other moral statements. Have several books available to show children the different morals that are present at the end of the story. Choose Aesop stories, or use stories familiar to the students and have them suggest morals to those stories.

Strategies/Skills: Brainstorming, making connections to real life situations, story webbing

Primary *LTM* component: *Cognition*

LESSON 6

"The Ant and the Grasshopper"

- Introduce Aesop's Fables and compare this genre to the nursery rhymes (refer to the history section). The main concept is to help students understand that just as rhymes were satirical in nature, were created by adults for adults, and mirrored the political events of the times with humorous chants, so also Aesop's Fables reflected the problems and political situations of his time with mini moralistic stories.

- Students will be reading many of Aesop's Fables, researching literature, and extracting issues from our present political agendas in society, in order to determine values that cause us to wrestle with the building blocks of our character. To help develop character, it is important to provide images of characteristics that we want our students to emulate. As an introduction to this lesson, read two or three of Aesop's Fables and ask the students to discuss what they consider to be the *moral*.

- Read "The Ant and the Grasshopper." Discuss the moral of this story: *Prepare today for the wants (needs) of tomorrow.* In groups of four, discuss and report to the class the resources that might be depleted in the future. What do you think our society needs to do today in order to prepare for the needs of the future? What can we, as individuals, do to prepare for the future? Place ideas on transparency. Groups report their findings to the class.

- Prepare a list of story characters, possible settings, possible problems, and possible solutions. The class will randomly choose one item from each of the four categories, and create a class fable using this unique combination. Encourage them to use magazine printed words and pictures. Students can choose to work individually or in pairs.

- For an additional activity, students can research or talk with adults or other students concerning things they can do to help preserve the earth's natural resources for the future.

- Have the students define the difference between character and characteristics. *Character* portrays the particular qualities or habits of an individual, while *characteristics* are the individual qualities or habits that make up one's character.

- Recall the fables read and make the distinction between character and characteristics. This could be done by creating a web on the chalkboard or on poster board.

- Brainstorm positive and negative characteristics, i.e.:

trustworthy	dishonest
respectful	rude
responsible	irresponsible
fair	spiteful
caring	callous
accountable	unreliable
sincere	deceitful

- Pass out a variety of Aesop's Fables either from library books or downloaded from the Internet: http://classics.mit.edu/Aesop/fab.mb.txt. Ask the students to research other fables that portray the characteristics mentioned and add to the list if necessary.

- As a home assignment or extended class activity, have the students research the animals in a matrix (see matrix template at end of unit) and match the animal with its dominant characteristic.

Strategies/Skills: Perspective, point of view, creativity, futuristics, cross impact matrix

Primary *LTM* component: *Problem Solving, Decision Making*

LESSON 7

Life, So Far . . .

- Share the fable "Hope for the Flowers" by Trina Paulus. Discuss the story with the group, eliciting individual ideas about the meaning of the story. If possible, secure a copy of an original story created by Cheryl Friberg, "A For Real Tale and a Heart in Search of . . . " This unpublished story is available by contacting Ms. Friberg at imafreebird@aol.com.

- Using a story-webbing outline, the students will create a fable that will reflect their life experience in which they learned a lesson. Students will be asked to consider what life has taught them . . . so far! List their ideas on transparency. Using what they know about fables, students will create several morals to accompany these life's lessons. Using a backward design in which the students know the moral before the story is written, students will create a story which has the selected moral as its ending.

- Using the matrix from Lesson 6 and the students' research findings, the class will work in small groups to collaborate their findings by sharing why they matched each animal with the particular characteristic(s) that its behavior portrays.

- The students will summarize their small group discussion for the whole class.

- Either on their own, with a partner, or in a small group, the students will use the information shared to construct their own fable using one of the animals and its dominant characteristic(s) reflected in the moral of the fable.

- Have the students share their fable by acting it out. The class determines the moral that was developed in the role-play of the fable.

Strategies/Skills: Analysis, decision making, risk taking, synthesizing, collaboration

Primary *LTM* component: *Interpersonal Communication*

LESSON 8

Character-US-STICKS, Character-THEM-STICKS

- Using their prior knowledge of animal characteristics, engage the students in a discussion of animal nature and human nature. What is the same? What is different? (i.e., Create a Venn diagram to depict this.)

- In a discussion, consider the following issues:

  How does the ability to choose affect our society?

  What role do rules play in our society?

- The above discussions should lead to topics such as: fairness, rights and responsibilities of and for all people, self-control, equality, justice, and so forth. Once the class discussion has formulated some ideas, create the following simulated activity. (You may want to let someone in administration know of this activity in case any of the students feel they are treated unfairly.)

1. Tell the students that they are going to participate in a simulated activity. It is important for every individual to listen and follow directions carefully.

2. Have the students close their eyes. Anyone caught opening their eyes will be removed from the simulated activity.

3. While students have their eyes closed (or were out of the room for recess or another class), set up two tables: the "US" table and the "THEM" table. At the "US" table place cheese, crackers, fruit, fruit juice, and other little goodies. At the "THEM" table place saltine crackers and water.

4. Pass out Popsicle sticks with half labeled "US" and the other half labeled "THEM" to the students in random order.

5. Tell the students that when they open their eyes they will have a stick on their desk, with either the word "US" or "THEM." They will go to the table that is labeled on their stick and eat the meal provided for them.

6. Students will have varying reactions. Observe the students' behavior.

7. Once they have experienced the injustice of this simulation, allow them to express their feelings and relate their experience with the simulation to the previous discussion of human nature. (Since it never stated they couldn't share, did the "US" table begin sharing with the "THEM" table? Why? Why not?)

8. We often categorize ourselves into "us" and "them." There are those who are "in" and those who are not. There are those who "have," and those who "have not." As humans, how can we use Lesson 8's characteristics in the experience of the two tables?

- Journal: How did you feel during this simulation exercise? What did you do or what did you not do that contributed to the experience of this simulation of human behavior? What characteristics (positive and negative) did you portray in this experience? What could you have done differently that would have changed the direction of the role-play?

- Students may be upset that they did not think to share with their "less fortunate" friends. Ease their guilt by reiterating that this was a *simulation* exercise; it was meant as a learning experience. If they learned something new about themselves, they are beginning to evaluate their own character and heighten their awareness to make different choices in the future with real situations.

- Read the fables "The Stag at the Pool," "The Trees and the Ax," and "The Soldier and His Horse." These stories deal with issues of being treated with respect, and treating others like you want to be treated. Remind them of the famous saying, sometimes known as the Golden Rule: "Do unto others as you would have others do unto you."

- Engage the students in a conversation that allows them to recall situations in life that are like the experience they just had, but are real situations, i.e., having cliques in school, ignoring others who are different from you, poverty in the world, and so on.

- Have the students create a fable that deals with the issue of an injustice in our society or in our school. This could be done individually or with a partner. Consider pairing an "US" with a "THEM."

- As a closing activity, read Dr. Seuss's *Yertle the Turtle*. This story contains the following quote: "I know, up on top you are seeing great sights, but, down at the bottom we, too, should have rights." Discuss this phrase as it relates to some issue the students are facing now.

Strategies/Skills: Simulation, creative writing

Primary *LTM* component: *Interpersonal Communication*

LESSON 9

"For Real" Tales

- Summarize the lessons that have been taught thus far in this unit involving nursery rhymes and Aesop's Fables. Remind the students that the original rhymes and fables were written for adults and reflected society's pressures and problems.

- Introduce a variety of fairy tales (see History of Fairy Tales). The students individually, as pairs, or in small groups read a variety of fairy tales from the library or Internet. A great book for analysis and reading of fairy tales is *Tales of the Brothers Grimm*, edited, selected, and introduced by Clarissa Pinkola Estes, Ph.D.

- Allow students to search fairy tales on the Internet. (The teacher may want to bookmark particular Web sites for the students in order to limit students' access to the Internet.) Check out the following Web site for folk and fairy tales: http://www.yale.edu/ynhti/curriculum/units/1984/4/84.04.07.x.html

- Have the students analyze these stories for common themes and characters and list them on the board or chart paper: i.e., good vs. evil; the orphan or poor child who rises to the top. List common characters such as the king and queen, prince and princess, wicked witch, step-mother, frog, dwarf, giant, ogre, dragon, knight, white horse, beauty, and beast. Facilitate the students in a discussion of how these fairy tales are mirrored in their own life experiences and personal growth by having them choose one theme or one character and tell why they are most like that character. Relate this information to a classmate, or write it in a journal.

- Ask the students to brainstorm other literary selections that contain similar themes of dealing with and perhaps overcoming life's obstacles from fairy tales or morals from Aesop's Fables (i.e., *Anne Frank, Bridge to Terabithia, Red Badge of Courage, The Outsiders, Anam Cora,* and so forth).

- Have the students journal some of the themes in their own real-life experience, then create their own "For Real Tale," i.e., "A For Real Tale and a Heart in Search of" by Cheryl Friberg.

- Allow the students to complete, illustrate, and share with their peers these "For Real Tales." With the students' permission, the stories can be published in a class book and shared with the school's library.

Strategies/Skills: Research, incubation, analysis, creative writing

Primary *LTM* component: *Cognition*

LESSON 10

"Happily EVEN After"

- Engage the students in a discussion of life as it is and life as it "ought" to be. How is this modeled in fairy tales?

- Fairy tales always seem to end, ". . . and they lived . . ." (allow the students to fill in "happily ever after"). Discuss how fairy tales have ingrained in us this image of "living happily ever after" and how we forget to put emphasis on the trials one has to overcome in life in order to live, "happily EVEN after."

Encourage a stimulating discussion that might include:

Ask the students if life experiences measure up to the fairy tale images of life. Why? Why not?

Ask the students what makes a hero. Do we need heroes and heroines in our lives? Why? Why not?

Discuss the difference between sports and entertainment heroes and heroines vs. the normal, everyday person next door hero or heroine.

Who are our heroes and heroines of the past? present? future?

- Now that students have discussed the ideas of heroes and heroines, have them create a profile of a hero or heroine.
- Look through magazines and newspapers, and cut out pictures of real-life heroes. Tell why you think this person is helping people live "Happily EVEN after." Create a class booklet of these pages.
- Using current issues, write a Nursery Mine, MeSop Fable, or For Real Tale that reflects today's political and moral society. The students may want to publish these for classroom or library use.

Strategies/Skills: Research, technical writing, imagery

Primary *LTM* component: *Cognition*

HISTORY OF MOTHER GOOSE

Inquisitive individuals have taken it upon themselves to investigate this folklore of jingles, rhymes, and the verbose ditties of an eccentric old woman named Mother Goose, and to delve into the oral history and historical genesis of these rhymes' creation. The true history of "Mother Goose" is vague. Intrigued by her wisdom and wit, those who believe in her existence can identify her origins to at least three possibilities:

1. The Biblical Queen: Queen of Sheba

2. From the medieval times with Charlemagne's mother, Queen Bertha, during the late 700s. Her nickname was "Queen Goose" or "Goose Footed Bertha" because it was believed she was either web-footed or pigeon-toed.

3. The most common American belief is attributed to Elizabeth Goose, whose last name could have been "Vergoose" or "Vertigoose." She lived in Boston during the Colonial era. It is believed that she occupied her children and grandchildren by using the chants and rhymes from her own childhood memories. It is believed that her son-in-law, Thomas Fleet, collected these rhymes in a book called *Songs for the Nursery* or *Mother Goose's Melodies*. However, these sources have not been authenticated by historical research. Mother Goose is usually depicted as being "old with a crooked nose and very large chin." Some say she wears a tall hat, possesses powers, rides a goose, and can sometimes be seen with an egg in her hand.

In 1697, there was a book published in France titled *Stories and Tales of Past Times with Morals* or

Tales of Mother Goose. It is also believed that John Newbery, a publisher from London, published the first edition of Mother Goose. This book reflected the Mother Goose as she is known today. The titles were similar to titles believed to have been printed by Thomas Fleet, *Mother Goose's Melody* or *Sonnets for the Cradle.* Although there is no copy of this 1760 text, a reprinted date from 1791, containing fifty-one rhymes in a small book with small illustrations, was located. A Boston publishing company enlarged this version in 1833, including new poems copied from the book of *Gammer Gutron's Garland,* in 1784.

It is believed that nursery rhymes were not meant for children. Believing these rhymes and riddles were created for adults, most have their roots in political satires or were used as spells to ward off superstitions.

Examples

"Baa Baa Black Sheep" refers to paying taxes. Peasants in the Middle Ages had to give one-third of their income to the King (master), one-third went to the nobility (the dame), and one-third was kept for themselves (little boy).

"Hey Diddle Diddle." Many versions for this rhyme abound. One is that it is a story about the stars. The dog is Sirus, the spoon is the big dipper, the cat could be Leo the Lion, and the cow, Taurus the Bull. (Anderson) Another version proclaims this rhyme to be apocalyptic in nature, foretelling of misfortune. Still another verifies it as England's royal court where Elizabeth I was often called "The Cat" because of the way she fiddled with her cabinet members "as if they were mice." The cow, moon, and her lapdog were known as characters in these court charades. The dish was Elizabeth's serving lady and the spoon was the royal taster who tasted food to make sure it was not poison. It is said that these two ran away and eloped.

"London Bridge" refers to the bridge of the 1800s over the Thames River, which replaced a wooden bridge built in 1209. That bridge was then replaced again in 1970. The 1800 replacement was moved and is now in Lake Havasu City, Arizona.

"Old King Cole." One interpretation is that this poem refers to a king by the name of Coel, whose capital was Colchester.

"Mary Had a Little Lamb." It is very possible that this rhyme is about a little girl named Mary Sawyer who nursed a baby lamb back to health. The animal, acting like a loyal pet, would follow her to school. It is believed that Mary attended the Redstone Schoolhouse. There is a Redstone Schoolhouse Society that is currently researching this information and related information and rhymes as well.

"Rock a Bye Baby" is attributed to a Native American tradition of hanging birch-bark cradles on tree branches.

HISTORY OF AESOP'S FABLES

Aesop is known for his proverbial sayings regarding one's experiences of life. Although Aesop's birthplace cannot be historically proven at this time, there are many Greek cities that try to claim his fame. Despite the nonhistorical traditions that surround this renowned character, there are some facts that have been established as true facts relating his birth, life, and death. Most scholars place his birth around B.C. 620. Born into slavery, he was owned by two masters, both inhabitants of Samos. Aesop's last owner allowed him to go free as a reward for his education and sense of wit. This action gave Aesop the ability to become vigorously interested in public concerns. By following his desire to learn and to teach, he traveled through many countries, ending up in the courts of Croesus. He is believed to have pleased his royal master, by conversing with the philosophers of the court. He made his home in Sardis, and Croesus would consult Aesop over difficult and fragile situations of the state. Aesop traveled to the small republics of Greece. He was also known to have gone to Corinth and Athens, telling and teaching his wise fables to help reconcile the people with the administrations of their respective rulers. However, due to the people's greed, Aesop refused to divide the gold brought from them under the command of Croesus. The townspeople executed him, even though he was Croesus' ambassador. The well-known adage, "The Blood of Aesop," became popular after the citizens who killed him were visited with a series of catastrophes until they made public restitution for the death of Aesop. There is a statue erected to Aesop's memory in Athens, Greece.

The histories of Mother Goose and Aesop both have their roots in the political agendas of the day. Mother Goose rhymes were known more for being satirical in nature, while Aesop's Fables were allegory statements, reflecting the political perils of his times.

HISTORY OF FAIRY TALES

According to Plato, a child who is exposed to stories, art, and music develops a love for virtue. Stories that are laden with virtuous acts attach themselves to a person's psyche and creative imagination. It is here that the moral fibers of one's character are born. It is in fairy tales that children first hear about heroes and heroines. To develop character, it is important to provide images of what society considers appropriate characteristics. It is also important to research the cultural aspects of fairy tales. Each culture has core values and archetypal themes of human development. The expression of such values may differ among cultures, but fundamental values such as honesty, respect, perseverance, tolerance, and compassion are not limited to any particular people, culture, or time period. Fairy tales were written for adults, and portrayed the emotional and psychological life/death cycles that are experienced across cultures. Fairy tales have survived for thousands of years despite the fact that the stories as we know them have been through more than one metamorphosis. Fairy tales are alive and well, and carry within their pages the unwritten stories of the human condition that transcend all cultures and traditions.

EXTENDED ACTIVITIES

- Have students select a favorite fable and act it out with the addition of props, music, rap, poetry, and so on. They may want to make a video and show it to the class.
- Write wise, moralistic sayings on popsicle sticks, i.e., *Better to give than to receive, Honesty is the best policy,* and others. Put these sticks into a bag or basket. The students will pull a stick and write a fable or story to go with the moral.
- Engage the students in a discussion of trust. Are all people honest and trustworthy? Should you trust all people? Why? Why not? It is important to stress that trustworthy people care enough to not harm you intentionally. Journal: Think of a person whom you trust with your thoughts and feelings. Write about what makes them so special to you. What is one thing you want them to know? Or consider this journal topic: Are you a trustworthy person? What are the characteristics you possess that make you trustworthy? Cite an example of a time when you were trustworthy.
- Engage the students in a discussion on respect. Discuss self-worth and the worth of others. How do good manners and citizenship fit into respecting others? Choose from these journal topics to write about: 1) What are some ways in which you have experienced others' lack of respect for you? 2) What slogan can you create to remind yourself and others about respect?
- View video clips of animals portraying human characteristics (*Bambi, Charlotte's Web, Stuart Little*). What do these characters teach us about life and the way we treat others?
- With freedom comes responsibility. Brainstorm a list of freedoms in your life. What responsibilities are attached to them? (e.g., You are able to go to a friend's house, but have to be home by a particular time.) Choose one of these topics: What are some excuses we

make in order to not have to be responsible? (i.e., I'm too tired, I forgot, and so forth.) What are you doing to take responsibility for yourself? If you could choose between living and working alone and doing anything you wanted or living and working with others and having to follow the rules, which would you choose?

- Fairness is usually defined by one's own experience with life. It stems from prior life experiences of comparing yourself to others and what others have said or done to you. Is there a difference between intentional and unintentional fairness? Why? Why not? Journal: What are some "bugaboos" in your life experience that seem fair, unfair? What about in our school, city, country, or world?

- Brainstorm other words for compassion: kindness, empathy, caring, and so on. Have each student decorate a small manila envelope with his or her name on it. The students take small index cards or pieces of paper and write a sentence for each student in the class that describes a time when that person was noticed as being considerate or compassionate of others, then sign their name. (The teacher may want to supervise this activity or construct a way to monitor each student's response to every other person in the class.)

- Engage the students in a discussion of citizenship. Define citizenship. Discuss the importance of commitment to a group. What about citizenship at home? What are other groups that we belong to where citizenship is important? Activity: Rewrite the Pledge of Allegiance without using the word: pledge, allegiance, republic, indivisible, liberty, or justice.

- Engage the students in a discussion of the meaning of this saying, "A chain is as strong as its weakest link." The students will use or create a game that can be an example of this saying, i.e., Jenga, or any other type of balancing wood block game. If possible, have students speak to a band director. Listen to a band session with each musician playing his part alone. This does not sound too professional; sometimes it doesn't even sound like the song. Then have the band play all together. Discuss the difference between the two experiences.

- Have the students write a story about a character, fictional or nonfictional, that reflects one of the characteristics discussed in this unit. They are not allowed to mention the characteristic. They have to develop this characteristic in the behavior and attitude of the character. The students read their stories to the class and the class states which characteristic is portrayed. Write a recipe for living the life you love in order to love the life you live so you may live "Happily EVEN After."

- Research sayings and slogans by "quotable" persons such as John F. Kennedy, Will Rogers, Mother Teresa, Martin Luther King, Jr., Helen Keller, Dr. Seuss, Maya Angelou, E. B. White. Create a book of quotations. If interested, students might want to illustrate these sayings.

- Search in children's videos and/or books for an individual phrase or sentence that could be placed in a book entitled "Lessons to Live By." Some examples:

  "I don't know when I'll be back, but be back I will!"—William Steig *Dominic*

  "I know up on top you are seeing great sights, but down at the bottom we, too, should have rights."—*Yertle the Turtle,* Dr. Seuss

  "You must be careful. Treat them carefully. They are PEOPLE."—*Indian in the Cupboard,* Lynne Reid Banks

The most positive benefit of this activity is to allow older students the joy of returning to children's books in search of these statements. They should delight in this activity.

Nursery "Mines," "Me"sop Fables, and "For Real" Tales Activity Resources

EENSY WEENSY SPIDER SAMPLE

The Eensy Weensy Spider went to the park one day
She looked around and found a seesaw
And she began to play
And the Eensy Weensy Spider then went on her merry way.

The Eensy Weensy Spider went to Hollywood
There he won a prize; a little tiny hood
Now the Eensy Weensy Spider never had bad luck
Until one fine day his little hood got stuck!

PETER PIPER TONGUE TWISTER

Peter Piper picked a peck of pickled peppers
A peck of pickled peppers Peter Piper picked
If Peter Piper picked a peck of pickled peppers,
Where's the peck of pickled peppers Peter Piper picked?

SAMPLE PERSONAL TONGUE TWISTERS

Amazing Anne ate an apple
At Alfred's American apartment
If Amazing Anne ate an apple at Alfred's American apartment,
how many apples did Amazing Anne eat?

Dangerous Dominick dug a dozen ditches
A dozen ditches Dangerous Dominick dug
If Dangerous Dominick dug a dozen ditches
How many ditches did Dangerous Dominick dig?

Challenging Chance chooses to chew chocolate cherries in a chair
If Challenging Chance chooses to chew chocolate cherries,
Just how much chow can Challenging Chance chew?

TWINKLE, TWINKLE EXAMPLES

Twinkle, twinkle little star
How I wonder who you are.
I dance and swim and write a lot
I like the things that I am taught!

Twinkle, twinkle little star
How I wonder who you are.
I am happy with my best friend
We share good times that will never end!

Twinkle, twinkle little star
How I wonder who you are.
Swimming and writing are my thing
And doing art makes me sing!

Twinkle, twinkle little star
How I wonder who you are.
I know a lot; I have good friends
My Mom and Dad's time for me never ends!

LITTLE JUMPING JOAN

(Iona Opie)
Here I am,
Little Jumping Joan
When nobody's with me,
I'm all alone.

OTHER EXAMPLES OF STUDENTS' WRITINGS

Dustin's dumb, dirty dog Digby
Dances and drools in the dark.

Beautiful Brooke bumped brown baboon blowing bubbles while biking backwards.
Beautiful Brooke bumped Billy Bunny's breadbasket and bonked brother Bob's baseball bus!

Little Miss Anne sat on a pan eating her pizza pie.
Along came a dog and sat on a log
Wagging his tail behind!

Little Miss Uncool sat on a toadstool eating her grits and cheese
Along came a ladybug that made her sneeze
It made her drop her grits and cheese!

Moo, Moo Brown Cow. Have you any milk?
Yes ma'am, Yes ma'am three quarts full.
One for the farmer, one for the store, and one for the little girl living on the first floor!

Bark, Bark Brown dog. Give me one of your bones.
No ma'am, no ma'am I do not give out loans.
These bones are for my family; my family needs food.
So go and get your own bones, and don't be rude!

NURSERY RHYME TRIVIA SAMPLES

What was white as snow?

Who could not help Humpty Dumpty?

What did the Farmer's Wife use on the Three Blind Mice?

How many blackbirds were in the King's pie?

What precious stone is the twinkling star like?

Where was Peter's wife?

What did Jack jump over?

What instrument did Little Boy Blue play?

What did Miss Muffet eat?

Where did the Old Woman and her children live?

Why couldn't the Eensy Weensy Spider get up the water spout?

What happened to the Old Man who snored?

SAMPLE MATRIX

	Little Boy Blue	Little Jack Horner	Eensy Weensy Spider	Jack and Jill	One two...
Ring around the Rosie					
Old Mother Hubbard					
Baa Baa Black Sheep					
Mary Had a Little Lamb					
Diddle Diddle Dumpling	X				

EXAMPLE OF MATRIX STORY (COMBINING DIDDLE DIDDLE DUMPLING AND LITTLE BOY BLUE)

Diddle Diddle Dumpling
Little Boy Blue
Went to bed
With his horn on his shoe.

Diddle Diddle Dumpling
My son John
Asleep in the corn
with no shoes on!

	Whales	Zebras	Squirrels	Sheep Dogs	Dolphins	Ants	Canada Goose	Chimps	Other
Responsibility									
Individuality									
Cooperation									
Compassion									
Discipline									
Friendship									
Honesty									
Courtesy									
Learning									

REFERENCES

Aesop's Fables: Illustrated Junior Library (1999). Drawings by Fritz Kredel. Grosset & Dunlap ISBN: 0-448-06003-5.

Boffomedia's Mother Goose Rocks! http://www.mothergooserocks.com/.

Estes, C. P. (1999). *Tales of the Brothers Grimm.* New York: Quality Paperback Book Club.

Estes, C. P. (1992). *Women who run with the wolves.* New York: Ballantine Books.

Garnett, P. D. (1999). *Investigating morals and values in today's society.* CA: Good Apple.

Gash, Amy. (1999). *What the Dormouse said.* N.C.: Algonquin Books of Chapel Hill.

Grumet, M. (1998). *Bittermilk: women and teaching.* Amherst: University of Massachusetts.

Hall, R. *The DNA of Fairy Tales: Their Origin and Meaning.* http://www.-theosophy-nw.org/ theosnw/world/general/ge-rhall.htm.

Hoberman, M. *Eensy weensy spider.* Little, Brown Publishers. ISBN: 0-316-36330-8.

Lester, J. L. (2001). *Sumptiously silly fantastically funny fables.* New York: Scholastic Press.

Opie, Iona. (Ed). (1996). *My very first mother goose.* Cambridge, Mass: Candlewick Press.

Paulus, Trina. *Hope for the flowers.* New York: Paulist Press.

Ramsburg, D. (1998). *Understanding literacy development in young children.* Available at: http://ericps.crc.uiuc.edu/npin/pnews/1998/pnew498/pnew498b.html.

Redstone School Research. *Mary had a little lamb.* http://www.standingstone.com/fisherweb/ schoolhouse.html.

Sanchez, T. R. (1998). Using Stories about heroes to teach values. Eric Digest, ED424190, http:// www.ed.gov/databases/ERIC_Digests/ed424190.html.

Sensenbaugh, R. (1996). *Phonemic awareness: An important step in learning to read.* Eric Digest, Edo-Cs-96. June 1996. http://www.indiana.edu/~eric_rec/ieo/digests/d119.html.

The real story of Itsy Bitsy Spider. (1990). Golden Book Video. Western: Racine, Wisconsin.

———, Core Essentials. (2000). Dept. of Education's Georgia Center for Character Education and the Georgia Humanities Council. www.coreessentials.org.

———, TeachingValues.com. http://www.teachingvalues.com.

ADDITIONAL WEB SITES FOR RHYMES, FABLES, AND FAIRY TALES

www.pacificnet.net/~johnr/aesop/

www.AesopFables.com

http://aesop.creighton.edu

http://www.iyedo.com/

http://www-personal.umich.edu/~pfa/dreamhouse/nursery/rhymes.html

http://www.zelo.com/family/nursery/index.html

http://www.geocities.com/EnchantedForest/Dell/3942/

http://www.fairytalescollection.com/Aesop_Fables/Aesop_biography.htm

http://www.oldlondonbridge.com/america.shtml

http://www.mothergoose.com/History/History.htm

Chapter Seven

The Art of Science

Originated by Jill LeMaire

Subject Area: Science

Grade Levels: 6–9

OVERVIEW AND RATIONALE

Science creative? You bet! This unit is designed to get students involved in the art of science. Students learn about science careers, participate in scientific discovery, explore scientific principles, and delight in scientific phenomena! The creativity of art is incorporated into daily science activities as students learn to mesh these seemingly discrepant disciplines together.

UNIT GOALS

- Students will incorporate both analytical and creative thinking to become more integrated thinkers.
- Students will realize that an interest in the artistic fields and an interest in science are not mutually exclusive.
- Students will develop better leadership skills through training in the four components of the *Leadership Training Model*.

The Art of Science *LTM* Activities

Cognition Activities:	*Interpersonal Communication* Activities:
• Science/art careers • Color clues • Double displacement activity • The physics of kite building	• Design a new puzzle • Dance of the electrons • ArachnaFUNbia
Leadership Training Model	
Problem Solving Activities:	*Decision Making* Activities:
• Magic H_2O • A different perspective • Colors, colors • Design a kite	• Create a protist • Animal empathy

LESSON 1

"Magic H₂O"

- Forced Choice. Students will be asked: If you were locked into a career in either art or science, which would you choose? Why? Have students stand in a straight row, one behind the other. On a teacher-designated signal (such as a hand clap), students move to the left if they choose art or to the right if they choose science. Those who stepped left would have an opportunity to explain why they chose art as a career. Those who chose science would also have a chance to explain their reasons. Make sure students aren't allowed to say, "I think the same as . . .". Require students to reword their reasons, or express them differently, so that you allow each student to express true feelings.

- Discrepant Event: (See explanation of this activity at end of unit). Students will observe a setup in which two jars filled with blue water are inverted and placed on top of two jars filled with yellow water. Index cards are positioned between the mouths of the jars. When the cards are removed, one column mixes and the other remains separate. Students must figure out exactly what was done to cause such results by asking questions that are answerable with a "yes" or "no" only, to gather data to support the inferences they make from their observations.

- Brainstorming: List adjectives describing what students have just observed on transparency.

- Poetry: Students will compose a poem of any style using all or most of the adjectives listed on transparency.

- Have volunteers share their poems with the class and describe the internal processes that led to these products.

- Students will be assigned to research careers in chemistry which also involve artistic endeavors (for example, perfumers). Students will be encouraged to consult the classroom text, other materials the teacher has provided, the school and/or public library, or the Internet. Each student can then select a career of interest that would combine art and science. They should describe the career, and prepare a brief job description or create a brochure enticing other students to consider this field. This activity may be completed as an individual or with partners. Information about science careers can be obtained at http://library.thinkquest.org/11465/morecareers.html.

Strategies and Skills: Inference, analysis, brainstorming, fluency, exploration, poetry

Primary *LTM* component: *Cognition*

LESSON 2

"A Different Perspective"

- To allow students to understand positive and negative space, have a glass that is half full of water. Ask: Is the glass half empty or half full? Boundary Breaker: "What if the sky were solid and the trees were empty spaces?" Entice the students to suggest other examples of positive and negative space . . .

- In order to depict positive/negative spaces, students will create Vegetable Block Prints. Block printing is all around us (on T-shirts, ties, dresses, furniture fabric, and draperies). Students can choose to use any root vegetable such as a potato, carrot, or turnip. Have a variety on hand for them to choose one or several. Directions for completing block prints are readily available in any art book. (See simple directions for block prints at end of unit.) Encourage them to experiment and take risks. Tell them to be aware of the concept of positive and negative space while they are composing their print.

- Read the description linking block prints to crystals, honeycombs, and other patterns in nature (see description at end of unit).

- Redirect students' attention to the answers to the boundary breaker posed at the beginning of class. Have them select any response and draw a picture depicting that "what if." Have them color in the negative space and leave the positive space white. Have each student think of at least three new words that would be needed in this new world of positive/negative space. Write a short poem using these words.

- Something to think about: Do you break down unfamiliar words into roots, prefixes, and suffixes and figure out what they mean that way? Can you think of a difficult word that you deciphered in that fashion? Bring it to class tomorrow and share it with us.

Strategies and Skills: Flexibility, originality, artistic synthesis, divergent thinking

Primary *LTM* component: *Problem Solving*

LESSON 3

"Can You Decipher?"

- Students will be asked to share any words they discovered from their homework assignment. Direct their attention to the importance of scientific word parts. This information is available in the reference section of most science books. (See examples at end of unit.) After studying these word parts, ask students to create a working definition of *protozoa* without actually looking up the word in a glossary or dictionary.

- A Parade of Protists. Students will research information on protists from their text, from teacher-selected materials, or by doing a Web search. (Any other word search for protists on the Web might also yield appropriate results.) Students should jot down their impressions, fleeting images, and analogies that occur to them as they view these protists. The students will discuss the meaning of words such as *heterotrophic, autotrophic, photoautotrophs, endosymbiosis, amorphous, cytoplasm, pseudopods, diatom, spirogyra, euglenophyta,* or any other terms the teacher deems appropriate for the study of protists.

- Create a Protist. Have students form three-person groups and force together root words, prefixes, and suffixes to form new protist names using the matrix. (See matrix at end of unit.) Once students have created several "new" protists, they should use the reference on word parts to describe their new animals and create an illustration of them. This activity can be done with a partner, or each group member can independently select one name and draw an imaginary protist. Example: a *chlorosphotosoma* would be a green-bodied protist that emits light. Students might enjoy guessing the name of the invented protist by examining the reference chart.

- Journal entry: Have students creatively describe in writing their first impressions of the magnified photographs of protists. Describe what these protists looked like. Analogies are encouraged.

Strategies and Skills: Application, analysis, artistic expression

Primary *LTM* component: *Decision Making/Problem Solving*

LESSON 4

"Puzzlemania!"

- Plate Tectonics. Define plate tectonics and show pictures of how the continents once looked. Relate how the supercontinent broke up. Information is available on a number of Web sites including http://www.pbs.org. Check under the section *Science and Technology TeacherSource.* (See general information on tectonics at end of unit.) It would also be desirable to secure a video on plate movement and earthquakes.

- Mosaics. Explain the connection between plate tectonics and mosaics—the fitting together of pieces. Give students time to create an original mosaic using found objects they have brought to class, or objects provided by the teacher. Encourage them to show color contrast as well as texture contrast. They should also name their mosaics. Display them around the room as students finish their designs.

- Design a New Puzzle. Lead a whole group CPS session in which students agree upon a new puzzle design they would like to market, or a new computer game they would like to suggest to a company utilizing the scientific information they have learned thus far this year. (See CPS instructions in Chapter Two.) Have each student write a letter to a toy company inquiring into the procedure for submitting a new puzzle or game design.

- Journal entry. "Can you think of another connection between some topic in science and some art form?"

Strategies and Skills: Analogical thinking, art techniques, group dynamics, synectics

Primary *LTM* component: *Interpersonal Communication, Problem Solving*

LESSON 5

"Dance of the Electrons"

- Students will play a game similar to Twister in that upon being assigned a role as an atomic particle, they will take their positions on a skeleton frame of an atomic model that will be printed on a large sheet of paper spread out on the floor. Information on elements and matter is available at www.4kids.com under the keywords: science/chemistry/matter or electrons. Encourage students to explore several sites to learn more and varied information concerning electrons.

- "The Dance of the Electrons." Have students work in groups and choreograph a stylized dance in which they imitate atomic energy. Have students reach a decision on how to split up.

- Use other creative media to represent the structure or movement of atoms.

Strategies and Skills: Application, communication, creative movement, problem solving, research skills, role-playing

Primary *LTM* component: *Decision Making/Interpersonal Communication*

LESSON 6

"Animal Empathy"

- Boundary Breaker: "If you were a famous scientist, what would you want to be known for?" Encourage students to share their ideas. Some scientists study animals, and their ability to adapt in the wild. Imagine that you are a scientist, and that you have developed a great understanding of animals.

- Read the following poem to students:

The Squirrel

Grabbing, hustling, storing nuts
The supply gets smaller every year,
Prickly, short fur hugging my body . . .
Cautiously I move on the ground,
Barely noticing the coming winter,
Or thinking of others who have no food.
The park—the warmth of my home in the oak tree—
This is my home

- After reading this original poem, or other poems about animals' responses to nature, ask students to discuss the poem. Lead students in a guided imagery to experience a storm through the eyes of some animal. Students should come to the realization that people and wildlife must coexist. The teacher will adapt this imagery activity to the abilities of the students. Read or describe in words a series of images for students to conjure in their minds. Use words that are open to interpretation to encourage a variety of answers to develop in each student's mind. Leave time between the phrasing of words for the students to visualize the images suggested.

- Students, with writing or sketching materials, will walk to a local park and find a comfortable spot to view nature. Give students time to record their feelings either in words, through drawings, or both. Encourage them to see nature through the eyes of an animal they might see in the park.

- Sensory Exploration. Have students take time to experience their surroundings using all five senses; for example, if they are experiencing the park as rabbits, they might nibble on grass. Encourage them to stay in character and not speak to their classmates. Notes should be jotted down as needed.

- Animal Stories. Upon returning to class, students will write and illustrate a story that describes the ways an animal might experience a storm, a hurricane, a tornado or earthquake, or the like. This could be an individual or a group activity. Their story could use their park experiences as source material. Display the illustrated artwork around the room.

- Have students search for a comic strip or a cartoon in which we see the world through the eyes of animals. Ask: Why do you think this theme is so prevalent in cartoons?

- Students write a critique of their poems in which they point out strengths and weaknesses. Include discussion on the level of empathy reached with the selected animal and the achievement of the desired poetry form. Encourage students to think about birds, spiders, and other wild creatures the next time they see lightning, thunder, rain. Where are the other "creatures" who might be feeling this storm?

Strategies and Skills: Building empathy, visualization, creative writing

Primary *LTM* component: *Decision Making*

LESSON 7

"Colors, Colors"

- Boundary Breaker: "What color is happiness?" Explain choice.

- Read to students some background information concerning color. (See information at end of unit.)

- Abracadabra Chemistry: Teacher demonstration of double displacement reactions. Information on this scientific activity can be found at http://www.chemtutor.com/react.htm# double.

- Students will follow along with information. (See information at end of unit.) Complete each portion of the directions. At this point they will be asked to look for a pattern and predict the products of the last two reactions. Color Perception: Have students record the color changes they observe in the reactions. Do they all perceive color in the same way?

- To underscore the differences in perception, students will have an opportunity to discover some interesting facts about someone who perceived things quite differently because of her ability level. Have them read an excerpt from the writings of Helen Keller. Copies of her writings can be found at http://www.afb.org. Look under the heading Helen Keller/ Archives/Helen Keller papers. Two that are of particular interest are entitled "Are We Wasters of Time?" and "An Apology for Going to College." In these two sample writings, students can recognize the depth of intelligence Keller possessed, and the tremendous odds she overcame. She is also quite comical in her writings concerning "a woman's place." Considering her limitations, do you think she perceived colors in the same way you did?

- The magic of colors: Put five or six purple cabbage leaves in two cups of water in a pot. Cover the pot and bring the mixture to a boil. Let it simmer on low heat for fifteen minutes. Let it cool, then pour the purple juice into a bowl. Squeeze out extra juice from the leaves with a wooden spoon. Put three tablespoons of white vinegar into a glass jar, three tablespoons of clean water into another glass jar, and one tablespoon baking soda and three tablespoons water into a third glass jar. Stir until the soda is dissolved. (This could be done at home.) Add two tablespoons of the cabbage juice to each of the three jars. WATCH THE COLORS CHANGE! (Vinegar will turn the juice red, baking soda will turn the juice green, and water won't change the color of the juice.) Red cabbage is an *indicator*. It changes colors when mixed with an acid or a base. Scientists can tell by this color change whether a substance is an acid (red) or a base (green). You can test some of the liquids you drink— soda, milk, lemonade—to find out whether they are acids or bases. If the cabbage juice turns the liquid reddish, it is an acid. If it turns it greenish, it is a base.

- Collage making: Students will create a tissue paper collage in which they actually "paint" with tissue paper where colors bleed together to produce new shades of color. (See directions for this type of artwork at end of unit.) A sample of collage artwork can also be found at www.kinderart.com. Students will write a journal in which they describe or name any new shades of color they produced in their tissue paper collages. What mood do these colors suggest? Another excellent source is Eric Carle's video about how he creates his books. This information can be accessed at http://www.eric-carle.com/makepic. html.

- Ask: "If you could paint the future, what colors would you use?" If possible, share with the class a clip from the Robin Williams movie entitled *What Dreams May Come* (1998). Show the part of the movie when Williams enters a landscape painting and walks through the colors. This portion of the film is about an hour into the film.

Strategies and Skills: Creative media, synectics

Primary *LTM* strategy: *Problem Solving*

LESSON 8

"Kites and Physics"

- Read "The Sky" information to students (see passage at end of unit). Have students think about colors and properties of the sky. Encourage them to research information about the sky on the Internet or using a teacher-provided source.
- Students will be directed to pursue an independent study project in which they construct a functional kite. This kite will be decorated in a way that pays homage to an individual. Make sure students understand the word "homage." Students may consult classmates, adults, or the teacher in the course of their study, but the final product should be a predominantly independent effort. Students will be encouraged to integrate the biographical information learned about the selected person with the decoration on the kite.
- Students will share their product with the rest of the class and explain its functional and creative design. Students should consider originality and innovation of the concept and overall visual design. The overall composition and elements of design (form/shape, color, texture, and line) should be thoughtfully and uniquely associated with the work, personality, ideals, and outstanding contributions of the individual.

Strategies and Skills: Independent study, problem solving

Primary *LTM* strategy: *Cognition, Problem Solving*

LESSON 9

ArachnaFUNbia

- Each student will pull a fact slip on spiders (see fact sheet at end of unit). Then she must go around the room questioning classmates and trying to match the subject of her fact slip with three other students whose fact slips deal with the same topic. The four-person group that is first to correctly match up its slips will be declared the winner. Continue until all fact slips are paired into groups of four. Each group reads the fact slips, and tells how they relate. Note: The categories listed are the suggestion of the writer. Students may be able to create other combinations and connections!
- Guest speaker—expert on arachnids
- Question and answer period
- Construct a replica of a spider's web as accurately as possible, using recognizable geometric shapes. Materials used can include thread and glue, glue on black construction paper, or some other medium the teacher accepts. Some students might be able to use a paint program on computer, for example.
- As a culminating activity for this science unit, students will invite parents and other adults to "The Art of Science" art show. Students will display their art and write brief explanations of the scientific phenomena they discovered during this exploratory unit.

Strategies and Skills: Categorizing, interviewing, research skills, teamwork

Primary *LTM* component: *Interpersonal Communication*

Additional Teacher Information

A section is added to the addendum that gives examples of additional activities that the students might be interested in exploring. The activities are divided according to *LTM* components. See activities at end of unit.

MAGIC H$_2$O

Materials Needed:

4 small jars

2 index cards

blue and yellow food coloring

hot water

cold (or tap) water

Directions: Have this display already set up before the students arrive so they do not see that you are putting different temperature water in each of the jars.

Put one drop of blue food coloring in each of two small jars and one drop of yellow in each of the other two jars. Add hot water to one of the blue and one of the yellow jars. Fill the other two jars with cold water. Place an index card across the top of each of the blue jars, invert carefully and balance each pair exactly. You should have both blue jars (top hot, bottom cold) on top of both yellow jars (bottom hot, top cold) with an index card separating them.

Explanation: Temperature affects the density of water. Cold water has less energy present, so cold water molecules are closer together. Therefore, more molecules of cold water will fit into the same amount of space, resulting in a greater density for the cold water and the opposite for the hot water. Because of the slight difference in density between the cold and hot water, warm water rises and cold water sinks.

Ask the students: What effect does a temperature change have on density?

VEGETABLE PRINTS

Materials Needed:

root vegetables such as carrot, turnip, potatoes

knives, fingernail files, or other sharp objects

tempera paint

brushes

newspaper

newsprint or other porous paper

water

paper towels

Directions for creating print art: Cut a root vegetable in half, making a flat cut. Dig out small parts of the vegetable with a knife or file to make a simple design. Remember that the cut-out areas do not show, so make your cuts fairly deep.

Apply tempera paint to the parts of the vegetable that stick out. Stamp your vegetable onto a piece of paper. (You might want to use scratch paper at first to practice making good prints.)

Notice that the design comes out backwards! This is a creation of positive and negative space. Experiment with different colors or multiple colors. Try arranging your print in repeating patterns.

PATTERNS IN NATURE

A crystal is a rigid body that is formed when particles are arranged in a repeating pattern. Repeating patterns of atoms, molecules, or ions are caused by bonding.

Consider the patterns on wallpaper or drapery fabrics. Notice how the pattern repeats on the fabric. A major difference between crystals and wallpaper is that the units in crystals are three-dimensional.

Finally, as a bonus, students should be encouraged to search the Internet or other source and make crystals.

SCIENCE WORD PARTS AND MEANINGS

a-	without	**aeros**	air
ad-	near	**arthron**	joint
bi-	two	**autos**	self
endo-	inner, inside	**chloros**	green
epi-	on	**cystis**	pouch
exo-	outside of	**maxilla**	jaw
geo-	earth	**morphe**	form
halo-	salt	**stoma**	mouth
hemi-	half	**stasis**	position
hydro-	water	**thallus**	green shoot
hyper-	over	**vestigium**	footprint
hypo-	under	**-cide**	killer
iso-	equal	**-cyte, -cyto**	cell
meta-	between, change	**-gen**	producing
micro-	small	**-logy**	study of
mono-	one	**-oid**	like
neur-	nerve	**-zoa**	animals

Encourage students to find more base words, prefixes, and suffixes to complete this list. A discussion should include words they know that contain these word parts (ex: thyROID, MONOnucleosis, MICROwave, and so on).

Have students notice that

1. a syllable with (-) after it indicates a prefix
2. a syllable with (-) before it indicates a suffix
3. a syllable with no (-) indicates a root or base

CREATE A PROTIST

Directions: Students should fill in the chart with prefixes and suffixes along the left axis, and root words across the top. Once the prefixes and suffixes are determined, new "words" can be formed.

Root words   ⟶

P R E F I X E S S U F F I X E S							

PLATE TECTONICS

PLATE TECTONICS involves the movement and interactions of the plates that make up the earth's surface. Scientists are studying where the plates intersect in particular because these areas can be at higher risk for earthquakes when the plates shift.

Evolution of continents:

Pre-pangaea
  supercontinent
    Broke up 545–600 million years ago

Pangaea
  Ural and Caledonian mountains formed
    400 million years ago

Pangaea Supercontinent
    400–200 million years ago

Laurasia
  northern supercontinent (North America, Europe, Asia, Greenland)
    200 million years ago—North America split from Eurasia
    60 million years ago—Greenland split off
    10 million years ago—Iceland split off

Gondwanaland
  southern supercontinent (South America, Africa, Australia, Antarctica)
    180 million years ago, Australia/Antarctica split off
    180 million years ago, India split off
    150 million years ago, Africa, South America split off
    80 million years ago, New Zealand split off
    40 million years ago, Antarctica split off

THE ENJOYMENT OF COLOR

Technically speaking, colors do not have meaning. However, past history has led people to associate color with feelings, power, and authority. Some examples are listed below. See if you can find other examples.

PURPLE signifies

  imperial royalty

  love and wisdom united (red and blue)

  sometimes an emblem of mourning once
    black is no longer worn

YELLOW signifies

  pure happiness, sunshine

  royalty

  treason, deceit, fear

GREEN signifies

    growth, life, and hope

    jealousy (green with envy)

BLUE signifies

    truth and wisdom

    quietness and sincerity

    constancy and loyalty

WHITE signifies

    light, triumph, innocence, joy

    divine power

RED signifies

    passion

    anger

BLACK signifies

    evil

    mourning

    error and annihilation

    structural strength

ABRACADABRA CHEMISTRY

We are going to experiment with DOUBLE REPLACEMENT REACTIONS.

$$AB + CD \rightarrow AD + CB$$

HINT: Think of each chemical formula as being made up of a first and last name.

1. $CuSO_{4(aq)} + NaOH_{(aq)} \rightarrow$ _____ + _____

   COLOR CHANGE? _____

2. $BaCL_{2(aq)} + Na_2SO_{4(aq)} \rightarrow$ _____ + _____

   COLOR CHANGE? _____

3. $FeCl_{3(aq)} + NaOH_{(aq)} \rightarrow$ _____ + _____

   COLOR CHANGE? _____

4. $BaCl_{2(aq)} + Na_2CO_{3(aq)} \rightarrow$ _____ + _____

   COLOR CHANGE? _____

TISSUE PAPER ART

Artists often work like scientists—they experiment with materials to discover certain effects. Sometimes it takes a lot of practice to learn how to use a particular art material or medium. You will be able to experiment with the medium of colored tissue paper in this activity.

Tissue paper comes in many bright colors. It is transparent, so it glows when light shines through it. Today we will "paint" with tissue paper by brushing white glue mixed with water over it. By tearing and overlapping the different colors of tissue, you can make the colors blend together to produce new shades of color. By crumpling or wrinkling the paper before gluing it down, you can add texture and varying depth of color.

Art Materials: white drawing paper; colored tissue paper; white glue (diluted with water); black waterproof ink pen; dark colored construction paper; newspapers (to cover work area).

Directions: Fill a sheet of white paper with a collage depicting a scene of your choice. Landscapes do well. Experiment by "painting" over various colors and shapes of tissue paper with a mixture of water and white glue. Try overlapping tissue sheets or crumpling them. Try not to get the paper too wet—it will tear.

Add dark tissue to create a strong contrast. Include a variety of shapes and colors. If desired, once the glue is dry, you can add patterns and details with black waterproof ink.

Display your finished piece on a wall or in a window and let your light shine through!

THE SKY

Look up at the sky . . . what do you see? BLUE? GRAY? Clouds? Actually, what you see is an illusion. It appears to have mass and light, but it doesn't have either. It only allows the sun's light to penetrate through it. It does not possess color, either. It only reflects it through particles in the atmosphere.

The clouds are water vapor drawn up from the earth, and as solid as they may appear, they are also an illusion.

Lightning is pure energy, yet it appears to be a solid. Another illusion.

How does the sky affect our moods? What happens to you when the sky is dull and gray? How about bright sunshine? How does your mood change when the barometric pressure drops to indicate an approaching storm? How do you feel when the sun is first peering on the horizon, indicating a new dawn? How do you feel when you witness the orange glow of an evening horizon?

FUNCTIONAL KITE

This kite will be very special. You are to choose any famous person, and pay homage to that individual on your kite. The kite should emphasize innovative design inspired by or representative of the work or personality of your selected individual. The construction should be conceived and designed in such a manner as to make suggested visual references to the character of your individual.

There will be no limitations on the size, color, texture, or imagery of your kite. The only requirement is that you will be asked to briefly describe in writing the reasoning for your design. Originality and innovation will be rewarded, as well as overall visual design. The overall composition and elements of design should be thoughtfully and uniquely associated with your selected individual. Oh, yes, and of course, the kite MUST be able to fly!

You may choose any famous person you like. You may have to conduct some research on that individual in order to gather ideas. Consult the library, teacher center, or Internet to gain information on how to construct a kite.

Good Luck—Happy Flying!!

FACT SHEET: SPIDERS

Teacher: Separate the following facts into individual "fact slips" and follow directions detailed in Lesson 9.

Spiders in the Amazon rain forest build webs about a meter across and five meters up in the trees to capture large flying insects.

Only about half of all known spiders actually spin webs.

The most well-known spider webs are the orbs. This is the most efficient type of web. The orb web is composed of a framework of strong lines within which radial strands connect the center of the web with the framework.

Trap-door spiders are so named because they build soft silken tunnels and cap them with hinged doors.

Spider silk may be as thin as a millionth of an inch across, and it can be stronger than steel.

Wolf spiders are expert hunters that use their large eyes to spot prey.

The golden-silk spider can easily be recognized by the tufts of hair on its legs.

Spiders help humans by eating vast quantities of harmful insects that might damage crops.

Only a very few spiders have venom strong enough to kill a person, and even those spiders are much more likely to make a person very ill rather than actually killing him or her.

Black widow venom contains four different poisonous components. They work by paralyzing the victim and then slowly killing the victim by damaging its nervous system beyond repair.

Brown recluse spider venom is poisonous.

The terrible reputation of tarantulas is unearned; their venom has virtually no effect on humans.

Tiny black spiders in Britain make little silvery webs in meadows. They are called "money spiders" because some believe they bring money or other good fortune.

E. B. White wrote a story about a spider called *Charlotte's Web*.

Dr. Thomas Muffet (1553–1609) believed spiders to be good remedies for many ills. His daughter, Patience, was the real-life "Little Miss Muffet."

The Spider Woman is said by Navaho legend to have passed the secret of weaving to their tribe through a Pueblo girl who lived among them.

EXTENDERS

Cognition:

1. Visit a lab and write a description of your experiences.
2. Interview a chemist.
3. Write a report on carbon dating.
4. Write a report on alchemy.
5. Explain the Periodic Table of the Elements to a fourth grader. Use language a young person can understand, or try using metaphors or analogies in your explanation.
6. Prepare a "Chemistry Dictionary."

Problem Solving:

1. Build a chemistry set using household items in place of test tubes, Bunsen burners, and chemicals.
2. Create a new element. Describe its uses, dangers, and other characteristics.
3. Find out how a crystal garden is made, and make one.
4. Find and demonstrate ways of purifying water.
5. Explain why soup reacts differently in different types of water.
6. Make your own toothpaste.

Interpersonal Communication:

1. Prepare an oral presentation explaining why you are for or against germ warfare, chemical warfare, and so on.
2. Write a letter to the editor describing the pros and cons of cloning or stem cell research.
3. Pretend you are a presidential advisor. Prepare and deliver your advice to the president on the topic on which you wish to give him advice.

Decision Making:

1. Make a scrapbook of newspaper articles about science discoveries. Share articles with the class.
2. Make a scrapbook of labels from household goods, citing common elements found in each. Create a unique "shopping list," using the scientific names of such common items as "sodium chloride" (salt) or "sucrose" (sugar).
3. Arrange for a person who has undergone chemotherapy to speak to the class.
4. Prepare a career booklet describing the various types of jobs that are available in the field of science.

Chapter Eight

Talking Dogs, Singing Frogs, and Chocolate Cows

AN ADVERTISING UNIT

Originated by Mikki Welsh

Subject Area: Advertising

Grade Levels: 6–10

OVERVIEW AND RATIONALE

The purpose of this unit is to expose students to the various types of advertising and the psychology involved in successful advertisement. Propaganda techniques, marketing targets, and creative endeavors are explored. The lessons develop strategies for the literary development of middle school and high school students. Students have many opportunities to explore the various avenues of advertising using a variety of media such as television, newspaper, magazines, and so on. Classes explore the tried-and-true methods of primitive copy setting as well as the modern use of computer-generated techniques.

Students learn to incorporate their unique ideas into creative advertisements for business as well as for personal reasons. Group work includes higher-level thinking, problem solving, communication, and decision-making methods to create original advertisements. They create personal portfolios that highlight their advertising research combined with their own business cards, jingles, and voice mail messages.

Before beginning this unit, the teacher should collect a wide variety of commercial advertisements, both in print and on videotape, as well as a list of on-line examples. Sample business cards and business logos should also be available. The teacher should arrange for a guest speaker—e.g., a marketing specialist from an advertising firm, someone from a local newspaper, or someone who creates jingles—to lend authenticity to the purpose of the lessons.

UNIT GOALS

- To introduce students to the vast array of advertising that is in their world, and to allow them to explore the psychology of successful advertising.
- To expose students to an amount of detail in advertising that they would not ordinarily experience.
- To encourage students to initiate enrichment activities with advertising.

Talking Dogs, Singing Frogs, and Chocolate Cows
LTM Activities

Cognition Activities:	*Interpersonal Communication* Activities:
• Explore uses and types of propaganda • Determine advertising strategies • Create paste-up displays • Generate computer ads	• Create personal jingles • Create television commercials • Create voice mail messages for businesses
Leadership Training Model	
Problem Solving Activities:	*Decision Making* Activities:
• Evaluate effective ads/commercials • Develop criteria for awards • Create a unique logo for a business • Future problems in advertising	• SCAMPER new and improved products • Develop marketing plans to target a specific audience • Create personal business cards • Create personal portfolios

LESSON 1

Propaganda

- Ask the students to name some common jingles (e.g., Like a Rock—Chevrolet; My, my, my, Toyota—Toyota car company; It's the real thing—Coke; Just do it—Nike). Ask what many jingles have in common (rhyming, alliteration, set to music, humor, catchphrases easily remembered). Students write personal jingles about themselves. Allow the class time to do so; then have them share their jingles. For example:

  Do Wop Diddy Diddy Do Wop Shoo

  I use the Internet to E-mail you!

- Have available a wide variety of advertisements. (Also, ask students to bring in any additional ads they find at home.) Divide students into groups of three to four. Give each group a varied assortment of printed advertisements. After allowing students to review various ads, say: "Imagine that you have been appointed to a committee to select the best advertisement of all time. Which 'classic' advertisements would you choose as the best, and why?" Allow the students to discuss their choices. Ask the students if they find the products being advertised particularly appealing. Tell the class that today we will be discussing some of the techniques advertisers use to make their products sell.

- Show on transparency, then distribute the handout on "Propaganda." (See notes at end of unit.) Discuss the various types of propaganda, having the students cite other examples of advertisements that use them.

- Show a teacher-made video (approximately fifteen minutes) of television commercials. Pause at the end of each commercial to ask which type(s) of propaganda occur in that commercial. Students should also be noting differences between printed ads and commercials. Ask: Which is more effective for various purposes? Justify.

- Explain to the class that they will be working in groups to create their own television commercials. Use a handout to explain the criteria for the activity in detail. (See examples at end of unit; other criteria may be added as appropriate.) Divide the class into groups of four.

Have each group randomly choose a type of propaganda. Tell the groups that they must first develop a product to advertise, and in order to help them do this, we will be using a cross-impact matrix. Use the sample matrix transparency to demonstrate. (See matrix at end of unit.) Next, have the groups brainstorm a brief list of their favorite products, and then use those products in a matrix. Finally, they should select one "new" product to use in their commercial.

- Before students continue working on their original commercials, demonstrate a technique advertisers use to sell a product: the "new and improved" ploy. Distribute a handout of SCAMPER (see handout at end of unit), and have the class select a product with which to work. Lead the class in using SCAMPER to make a "new and improved" product (for example: a spoon).

- Ask the students to look through magazines or newspapers at home for advertisements that use the types of propaganda discussed and bring them to class the next day. Also, ask students to bring in materials that they would like to use as props or in creating props for their commercials.

- Ask students to begin researching the cost of 1) printed advertisements, 2) television advertisements, and 3) radio advertisements. This research could be done for extra credit or expanded into a separate lesson in math.

Strategies/Skills: Critical thinking, analysis, boundary breaker, guided discussion, synectics, creative thinking

Primary *LTM* component: *Cognition*

LESSON 2

Advertising Strategies

- Students share with the class the advertisements they brought from home, explaining which types of propaganda are used. If necessary, share teacher-collected advertisements. Create commercial story lines, which can be incorporated into a script. Determine appropriate props and begin rehearsing.

- During group work on their scripts, remind students to consider dialogue, facial gestures, hand and body movements, settings, and incorporating appropriate information during a specified time frame.

- Once groups have completed their scripts, direct them to begin creating props and/or costumes for their commercials, using materials provided by the teacher or other materials that they have brought from home.

- Allow groups to begin rehearsing their commercials. Encourage them to edit their scripts as needed at this stage. For example, students could select one group member to serve as "director," determining overall effectiveness and suggesting alternate solutions to improve commercial appeal. Also encourage groups to use video equipment to critique and revise their work in progress.

- Have individual group members rate their performances within their groups. Ask one member of each group (perhaps the director) to share what the group has accomplished and discuss any obstacles they have encountered. Encourage other groups to offer possible solutions.

- Remind the class they will be performing and (if possible) videotaping the commercials the next day, so they should bring in any costumes or materials that they will need.

Strategies/Skills: Creative writing, analysis, art, creative dramatics, group dynamics

Primary *LTM* component: *Interpersonal Communication*

LESSON 3

Evaluating Effective Ads/Commercials

- Divide the class into small groups (different from those working on the original commercials). First, each group will browse through a collection of magazine advertisements and select one that they believe is the best. Then, the groups may share their selections and explain why they have chosen them. Finally, the entire class must come to a consensus on the one "best" advertisement and select one student to explain the choice.

- Before enacting the commercials, the students will develop criteria for evaluating them. Explain that after the enactments, there will be an awards ceremony similar to the Cleo Awards, given to "real" advertisements. Brainstorm categories, such as "Best Performed" or "Most Creative," and then select favorite categories (at least as many as there will be commercials, preferably more to allow for leeway in selecting winners for the categories).

- Divide the class into as many groups as there are categories (again, the groups should be different from those enacting the commercials). Have each group create an appropriate "trophy" for the category.

- Students return to their commercial groups and prepare to perform the commercials. Each group will perform for the class, while another student videotapes the enactments. Instruct the remaining students to act as an audience, pretending that they are at home watching television.

- Once all of the groups have completed their performances, students will preview them on videotape, pausing at the end of each commercial for the class to constructively critique each group effort. Next, they are to act as judges for the Cleo Awards. Remind them of the categories of awards they have developed.

- Teacher (or award group) announces winners of the various categories (each commercial could receive an award if appropriate).

- Have the class stage an awards ceremony to administer their "trophies." Encourage the students to "ham up" their roles as presenters and receivers. Presenters should explain why the group is receiving the award. Elaboration and glowing praise are recommended.

Strategies/Skills: Group dynamics, brainstorming, art, creative dramatics, evaluation, analysis of student commercials, application of student-developed criteria

Primary *LTM* component: *Problem Solving*

LESSON 4

Marketing Techniques

- Students will view several different magazine advertisements and ask for each, "What sort of person might be attracted to this advertisement? How do you know?" This lesson will look at ways in which advertisers focus their efforts on particular segments of the population.

- Provide the students with as many resources on advertising as possible. Divide the class into small groups and tell each group that they are to use the resources to define what advertisers mean by the term "market" and some of the methods that they use to determine a market. Ask each group to share its results, and have the class determine a final definition and a list of ways for determining a market.

- Before students can develop a market survey, they need a product. First, the class will choose one of the original products used in their television commercials, or perhaps develop a new product. Then, the students return to their groups and brainstorm a list of questions they might ask to help them determine a market. Each group should select and share three of their questions. The entire class will then decide which questions to include in the survey, reminding them to limit the questions to a tolerable number, since many consumers quickly tire of tedious surveys. (Cite the example of telephone marketers calling your home during dinner.)

- Station the students at high-traffic areas of the campus to collect as many responses to their survey as possible in about thirty minutes. (Or, if the product would appeal to adults, have the students survey school adults, family members, and/or neighbors.)

- In the classroom, students compile their results. Guide the students in looking for trends in the data so they can develop market reports based on any discovered trends. Have each group select one student to present its report.

- Students will develop a marketing plan based on their reports. Divide the class into small groups and assign each group one type of advertising media (e.g., TV, radio, billboards, newspaper, magazine, bus or train station, park bench). Each group should develop a concept for an advertisement in their media, targeting the market as determined. Add a visual graphic.

- Groups will present their proposed campaigns, using their visual display.

- Students are asked to bring in copies of photographs and pictures that they would be willing to cut up and use to create an advertisement for the following lesson.

Strategies/Skills: Art, creative dramatics, evaluation, application

Primary *LTM* component: *Decision Making*

LESSON 5

Paste-Ups and Copy/Careers

- Students will work in groups to look through the magazine advertisements and choose the ones that they believe were the most complex to create. Ask them to explain their choices. Tell the class that this lesson focuses on a few of the techniques that are used in producing printed advertisements.

- If possible, invite a guest speaker from the newspaper or an ad agency to visit the class to explain about layout procedures. If this is not possible, the teacher will need to devote time to show students how to complete an ad "the old-fashioned" way, before computers.

- Distribute and review the paste-up handouts demonstrating the techniques with small pieces of art. (See handout page at end of unit.) Explain terminology, and allow students to refer to handout sheet often until the terms become familiar. Students will make their own advertisements using a *paste-up*. Instruct them to 1) make a printed advertisement for any product that has previously been developed in this class, 2) develop an entirely new product, or 3) create a paste-up about themselves. Hand out paper and old items such as magazines, catalogs, and calendars, and let the students take out any pictures that they have brought from home. Ask the students to look through the materials and use them to develop a *thumbnail sketch*.

- Once students have developed their thumbnail sketches, have them begin turning them into *comps,* using the techniques demonstrated earlier. Encourage them to begin thinking of copy for their advertisement as they work. Assist students in using the techniques as needed, but encourage students to find their own solutions to difficulties as they arise.

- Once the students have completed the art, tell them that we are ready to work on their *copy.* Call attention to the copy handouts (see handout at end of unit), again demonstrating the techniques with small pieces of copy. Inform the students that the old way of laying copy was to either paste-up letters photocopied from a font book, or mount purchased letters that came pre-glued. The modern way of producing both art and copy is with the use of computers. Explain that students will be using a combination of methods: they will type their copy with a word processor, adjusting the font and size as necessary, and then apply the copy as if it were art. After planning, allow the students to develop their copy on a computer, experimenting with the effects of various fonts, styles, color, and other attributes.

- Once the students have produced and printed their copy, have them apply it to their paste-ups. Again assist in the techniques, but encourage the students to use creative problem solving techniques.

- Students will present their comps to the class, explaining any obstacles they encountered and the methods they used for solving them.

- Have the students reexamine the advertisements that they believed to be complex at the beginning of class. Ask if they can now see how these might have been created.

- If possible, the guest speaker could also discuss different careers in advertising. To make the speaker's visit most productive, students should make a list of questions that they would like to ask the speaker, whether on an advertising process or on career opportunities.

Strategies/Skills: Analysis, art, creative writing, creative problem solving, questioning

Primary *LTM* component: *Problem Solving/Decision Making*

LESSON 6

Non-Media Advertising

- Show the students several examples of non-media advertisements (e.g., office letterhead, business cards, personalized stationery) and ask them what differences they see between these and other advertisements they have viewed. Explain that these advertisements are called "non-media" advertisements. Ask students what "media" means, and then develop with the students a definition of "non-media."

- The class should brainstorm other possible non-media advertising, listing responses on transparency. Have available several "logos" from local and/or national companies.

- Ask each student to develop a concept for a business, a *thumbnail sketch* for an appropriate symbol, and a logo for their business. The students will then develop their thumbnail sketches into *comps* using the techniques learned in the previous lesson.

- Have each student present his design, explaining the concept of his business and why this design is appropriate for that business.

- Each student will create a business card, which can be produced on a computer program, or by hand on card stock. The card may list the student as "president," "CEO," or some other executive designation, for the business. Encourage creativity and unique design.

- Finally, each student will develop a unique message for the answering machine, voice mail, or cell phone messaging for the business. Write the message, record it, and then share it with a partner or with the class.

Strategies/Skills: Analysis, brainstorming, art, presentations

Primary *LTM* component: *Interpersonal Communication/Problem Solving*

LESSON 7

The Future of Advertising

- Dim the lights. Ask the students to relax and close their eyes. Then say, "Imagine it is the year 2500. You are in a vehicle moving down a roadway. As you travel, you notice all sorts of advertisements. Take a moment as you are moving to observe the various types and appearances of these advertisements." Allow time to do so, and then have them write down what they saw. Next, have them share their images. Tell the class that the focus of today's lesson will be on their concept of the future of advertising. Inform the class that there are certain controls on advertisements today. For example, ads for cigarettes and hard liquor are not permitted on television or in magazines. Ask the students to suggest what controls, if any, should be imposed on advertisements and why. Encourage other students to agree or disagree and to support their arguments.

- Students research the topic of advertisement control, and hold a debate on the issue.

- As a class, develop a web of future events, beginning with one trend and expanding into different levels of consequences. This technique is used to suggest possible consequences of a particular trend or action.

- Ask the class to speculate how controls on advertising might change in the future, reminding the students that our values are constantly changing. Ask, "What might happen in the future that would force us to reassess our beliefs about ethical advertising?" List responses on the overhead projector. Then, divide the class into small groups. Have each group list possible problems related to advertising controls that might result from these changes.

- Each group should select one of the problems on which to work. Have each group state their problem in solvable form and then share their question with the class. Brainstorm a list of solutions to their question, encouraging them to continue searching for solutions even after they initially begin to slow in their idea production. Many students learn to seek only one answer to a problem, and this activity will encourage them to seek many answers, and then select the one that best suits the criteria.

- Using the CPS process as described in Chapter Two, have the groups suggest four or five ways by which to evaluate their solutions and choose eight to ten of their solutions with which to work. Instruct them to rate each of their solutions with their chosen criteria and ultimately choose a solution to their problem.

Strategies/Skills: Futuristics, imagery, prediction, future problem solving, presentation, evaluation

Primary *LTM* component: *Problem Solving, Decision Making*

LESSON 8

Advertisement Displays/Performance Evaluation

- Explain a *portfolio* to the class, citing examples and purposes of a portfolio.

- Then say, "The best advertiser in the world is a man named John Q. Advertising, and he is putting together his portfolio. He has created something for every type of advertising. Which current or recent advertisements are in Mr. Advertising's portfolio?" Encourage students to suggest items for Mr. Advertising's portfolio in each type of media and in non-media advertising.

- Explain that, when people seek jobs in an advertising agency, they must present portfolios to demonstrate their skills. Students do the same to demonstrate the skills that they have learned in this class. Have them collect the various pieces of advertising they have created (including the scripts for their commercials, their market analyses and reports, and their jingles and business cards). Ask them to write two paragraphs about each: one explaining the process by which it was developed, and one evaluating the work. Be sure to tell the students that they may have a peer edit their paragraphs, or they may ask the teacher to do so.

- Ask the students to create one more piece of advertising. This will be their "masterpiece," the piece that will surely land them a position in an advertising agency. Explain that they may choose any form of advertising and any available materials, but they are to work independently to create their masterpieces. Encourage students to be resourceful and show their creativity in order to "sell" themselves.

- Once the students have completed their masterpieces, have them compile their portfolios using their pieces, paragraphs, and materials provided for binding the portfolios using pasteup techniques. Last, allow time for the students to share their best pieces with the class and explain their choices. Ask the students to leave their portfolios for the teacher to review.

- Invite community members, parents, media executives, and others to a presentation/viewing of the advertising portfolios. Create a display in the library.

Strategies/Skills: Boundary breaker, creative writing, evaluation, art

Primary *LTM* component: *Decision Making, Problem Solving*

PROPAGANDA

Propaganda: the spreading of information or ideas to persuade people to be for or against something

Purposes of Propaganda:

to get attention

to show advantages

to create an emotional need

to persuade an audience

to seek action

Types of Propaganda:

BANDWAGON: Suggesting you do something because everyone else is doing it

TESTIMONIAL: A famous individual recommending something; also called an endorsement

TRANSFER: Associating an idea or product with something or someone you already feel positive about so that you will transfer those positive feelings to the idea or product

REPETITION: Repeating the name or catchphrase to help you remember it

EMOTION: Using words that arouse emotions rather than informational words

NAME CALLING: Degrading the competition to make your product seem more appealing

FAULTY CAUSE/EFFECT: Saying something will happen if you do as recommended when there is no relationship between the event and your actions

COMPARE AND CONTRAST: Comparing two similar products or ideas to convince you that one is better than the other

BASIC APPEALS: Appealing to human needs such as food, shelter, less work, greater comfort, and so forth

PLAIN FOLKS: Winning confidence by appearing like ordinary folks; used especially by politicians

As each type of propaganda is described, students should be able to cite examples of television or magazine ads they have seen that fit this description.

ORIGINAL TELEVISION COMMERCIAL

- Your group will randomly select a type of propaganda. Your job will be to write an original televison commercial to advertise a product using the type of propaganda you chose. Your group will also act out the commercial for the class. You may include other types of propaganda, but you should focus primarily on the type you've selected.

- Your group will develop a hypothetical product to use in your commercial. Consider a unique and clever name or slogan.
- The use of props is encouraged.
- Every member of the group must participate in the enactment of the commercial.
- The commercial should be forty-five seconds to one minute long.
- You must submit a written script at the time of your presentation.
- Your commercial will be evaluated using the following form:

1. Uses given type of propaganda	1	2	3	4	5
2. Produces a script	1	2	3	4	5
3. Originality	1	2	3	4	5
4. Creativity	1	2	3	4	5
5. Teamwork	1	2	3	4	5

SAMPLE MATRIX

Forced choice: A new way of creating new things by forcing together existing things. For example: peanut butter and chocolate!

	peanut butter	tomato sauce	chicken	watermelon
ICE CREAM				
WAFFLES				
FLAVORED CHIPS				
CRACKERS				

Of course, you can choose other things to force together unique and interesting combinations. Encourage the students to create unique combinations with other choices. Companies pay large salaries to those employees who create new products.

S.C.A.M.P.E.R.

S.C.A.M.P.E.R., a system developed by Robert Eberle (1977), is designed to enhance creative thinking. The exercise is designed to allow the students to identify modifications, changes, or adaptations to products; increase flexibility; and develop new ideas.

*S*ubstitute   What other ingredients or materials could we use?

*C*ombine   How can we combine parts or ideas?

*A*dapt   What else is like this? Could we change or imitate something else?

Modify	What can we change? Could we make it bigger?
magnify	Stronger? More frequent?
minify	Smaller, more compact, lighter, less frequent?
Put to other uses	How can we use it in another way?
Eliminate	What can be eliminated or omitted? Are all parts necessary?
Rearrange	Could we use a different sequence? Interchange parts?
reverse	Do the opposite? Turn it upside down, backwards, inside out?

ADVERTISING TERMINOLOGY

Advertisers use a certain type of jargon when referring to their work product. Most ad agencies currently use computers to draft their ads instead of the old fashioned cut-up and paste-up methods. However, there are still instances when an ad representative needs to produce a layout, a comp, and a copy to display for the customer. The following are definitions for various terms applied to advertising.

Paste-up Mechanical:

A work in progress form of a printed advertisement

Grades of Paste-ups:

thumbnail—small, rough sketches of an advertising concept
layout—a hand drawn but actual size concept
comp—short for "comprehensive"; used to show clients what the final product will look like
mechanical—a finished paste-up; ready for reproduction

Copy:

Text (wording) of an ad as specified by the customer or suggested by the ad representative

ADVERTISING WEB SITES

The following Web site might be helpful to both the teacher and the students.

http://www.adassoc.org.uk

In addition to the above site, you can find information on-line at the following site: http://www. goobig.com/. This is a free on-line encyclopedia. Type in *advertising* to browse definitions, slogans, types of advertising, and a list of slogans by product. Caution for teachers: One of the links is *Sex in Advertising,* which may be inappropriate for your students.

Chapter Nine

From Babe Ruth to Breadlines: A Historical Perspective

Originated by Bobbi Marino

Subject Area: Social Studies

Grade Levels: 9–12

OVERVIEW AND RATIONALE

This unit is designed to teach students the art of political cartooning while focusing on two colorful periods in American history: the Jazz Age and the Depression. Students are given an opportunity to learn about cartooning in general, then to discover the part political cartooning has had in historical references. Through cartooning, students learn creative as well as critical thinking skills while delving into historical records and artifacts.

UNIT GOALS

- To teach students the process and interpretation of political cartooning, focusing on the use of symbols, analogies, and caricaturing.
- To acquaint students with the period of the 1920s, focusing on cultural heroes, the roles of women, and advertising.
- To create student understanding of the effects the Great Depression had on families, and to appreciate the role of photographic images in history.

From Babe Ruth to Breadlines *LTM* Activities

Cognition Activities:	*Interpersonal Communication* Activities:
• Political cartooning • Research of historical figures	• Symbols, analogies, caricatures • Interview with older Americans • Photo analysis discussions
Leadership Training Model	
Problem Solving Activities:	*Decision Making* Activities:
• Heroes • Advertising activities • Superheroes	• Analysis and comparison of cartoons • Women of the 1920s

LESSON 1

Political Cartooning

- This unit should begin with a general discussion of the events that took place in the 1920s and 1930s, including Babe Ruth and breadlines. Students should be shown photos, trade books, encyclopedias, videos, and Internet sites to give them a glimpse of what life was like for persons living during those two decades. They should begin searching for someone they know who would have been their age during that time period. If possible, the teacher could arrange for one or more adults to come in and speak about that time period. Pique the students' interest into this special time in American history.

- Begin with a discussion about humor—what makes us laugh, what are some different types of humor, what are some popular cartoon characters, and so forth. Students should be free to discuss current cartoon strips and to enjoy sharing jokes with one another.

- Since this unit covers cartooning, students might fear that their lack of artistic skills will keep them from being successful. Allay their fears, telling them that they can create cartoons using stick figures or cut-out figures from other sources, or get a friend to draw pictures using their ideas. *It is the message the cartoon conveys that is most important.*

- To help students make connections with historical events of the '20s and '30s is not an easy task. This unit seeks to use political cartooning as a way for students to creatively explore this important time in American history. There are three basic concepts necessary for political cartooning: 1) symbols, 2) analogies, and 3) caricatures. Initial exploratory activities dealing with symbols will include the following:

  1. Political parties are found in many nations throughout the world. The United States has two major political parties. Find the symbols that represent each party and tell how each symbol originated.

  2. We encounter symbols in our lives daily. Some we take for granted. Draw or name as many different symbols as possible that deal with religious issues such as church, prayer, and differing beliefs.

  3. Draw symbols to represent things dealing with education.

  4. Draw or illustrate symbols for the economy.

  5. Sometimes a logo becomes synonymous with a specific business. Name as many symbols as you can think of that represent specific businesses (e.g., Golden Arches—McDonald's).

  6. How many symbols can you conjure up that represent our country?

- To introduce students to cartooning, attempt to help the students to become more observant. To do this, arrange students in pairs. Let them stare at each other for one minute, noticing the details and intricacies of each other's faces. Then have them draw their partner's faces with their eyes closed. (Some students are intimidated by required art projects, and closing their eyes should "free them" from intimidation.) The drawings generally come out as humorous and creative "Picassolike" images. After showing each other and the class the finished products, have them draw cartoon balloons above their own faces and write captions to fit them. Post these around the classroom.

- Humor can be used as a way of conveying important messages. Brainstorm "humor." Develop a checklist of what students think is funny. If possible, categorize these responses.

- Use samples of cartoons that have been collected on overhead transparencies to explain cartooning. Question students as they view cartoons and allow them the opportunity to discuss the themes of the cartoons or ask questions about them. Explain the format of cartoons.

- Editorial cartoons attract the most attention when they are simple. Sometimes one word or one symbol sends a powerful message. Create a cartoon using only one symbol. (See examples at end of unit.)

- Imagine that you can travel back in time. What place would you choose to visit, and who would you like to be? Keep this historical figure in mind as you begin to formulate a cartoon of your own. Have students tell the class whom they chose and why.

- Students focus on the historical figures they chose and research these persons and their time periods in order to develop ideas.

- Each student must tell a short joke or tell about something she thinks is funny. Discuss others' responses to this humor.

- Students should bring in as many examples of cartoons as they can for the duration of the unit.

Strategies/Skills: Observation, brainstorming, boundary breaker, forced choice, creative thinking

Primary *LTM* component: *Cognition*

LESSON 2

Symbols, Analogies, and Caricatures

- Have the following materials available for the students: political cartoons, newsprint, white and colored paper, news magazines, samples of symbols, analogies, and caricatures. The goal of this lesson is for students to investigate symbols, analogies, and caricature in cartoons.

- Have students think of words to complete these phrases: Being a pencil is like . . . . Being a hamburger is like . . . . Being a Harley-Davidson is like . . . . (Choose other phrases if they fit better with your students). Then give each student a sheet of colored paper to finish this statement: Being a teenager is like . . . . Display the finished products in the classroom.

- In groups, list all the symbols they can think of that deal with religion, education, the United States, economics, sports, and/or other categories. Each group will create lists and post them in the classroom for future reference.

- Ask students: What is an *analogy* and how can it be used in editorial cartooning? Explain *analogy*. With a partner, go through magazines and find political cartoons that use some type of analogy. Cut them out and be prepared to share your findings with the rest of the class.

- Working with a group, use the 2000 presidential election (or some recent news event) as your topic to write three analogies. Share with the class.

- Ask: "If you could change one thing about yourself, what would it be and why?" Let students explain their answers. Was the change physical, social, or emotional? Most likely, the students chose something physical. Was it a trait that could be caricatured? Discuss caricatures.

- Using the cartoons, check for examples of caricature. Show other examples of caricature. Students will then be given an opportunity to create a cartoon using caricature. Remember to exaggerate physical features.

- On a sheet of paper to be turned in, finish this statement: "When I am hungry, I feel like a . . ." You may answer in words, symbols, or drawings.

Strategies/Skills: Analogies, boundary breaker, symbolism, collaborative learning, creative thinking

Primary *LTM* component: *Problem Solving*

LESSON 3

Analysis and Comparison of Political Cartoons

- Have the following materials available for students: white and colored paper, cartoon magazines (e.g., *Cartoon News* or *Mad*), comics from newspapers, teacher collected copies of cartoons, and handouts of "Cartoon Analysis" worksheet and "Scavenger Hunt" game, available from the National Archives and Records Administration Web page available at www.nara.gov/education/teaching/analysis/cartoon.html.
- Allow the students to delve further into caricatures through some or all of the following activities:
  1. Cartoon and caricature are two very interesting words. Do you have any idea of their derivation?
  2. Ask an art teacher to demonstrate caricaturing for the class.
  3. Explain the relationship between caricatures and negative stereotyping.
  4. Go to http://www.cartoonews.com to find the prominent people caricatured on their covers. Tell who they are and why they were chosen.
  5. Find caricatures of three different American presidents.
  6. If you dare, draw a caricature of your favorite teacher(s). First get permission. Be sure to show it to the lucky teacher when you are finished. Share his/her reaction.
  7. Using caricature(s), make a cartoon that highlights an event in Louisiana politics.
- At the end of this lesson, each student should have created an original cartoon utilizing symbols, analogies, and/or caricature. Ask the students to imagine that they are on a panel of judges who will give a prestigious award for cartooning. Divide the class into groups of four to six students who will be designated as panels of judges. Before winners are selected, students must first develop criterion lists by which the cartoons will be judged. Using the criteria, each panel selects a first, second, and third place winner by written vote from the panel. Have them share their criteria and list of winners with the class.
- As a group, brainstorm current events. Tell students to individually create cartoons using the historical figure they chose to research in Lesson 1. To create their cartoon, they may use their own artwork, stick figures, symbols, or cut-out characters from the newspaper comics. Have them try to place their character into one of the current events that the group listed.
- Using *Cartoon News* (see Web site address above), students choose three cartoons and analyze them using the Cartoon Analysis worksheet. (See sample worksheet at end of unit.)
- Using the same three cartoons, students complete the Scavenger Hunt sheet. (See sample scavenger hunt at end of unit.) They have one minute to tell why they believe they are becoming good political cartoonists.
- Make this your thought for the rest of the day . . . HEROES.

Strategies/Skills: Comparison/contrast, analogies, analysis

Primary *LTM* component: *Problem Solving/Decision Making*

LESSON 4

Heroes

- Brainstorm (put words and phrases on transparency)

  a) What does the word "hero" mean?

  b) Who are the "heroes" of today?

- Boundary breaker: Who are your own personal heroes?

- Show a film, sections of a video, Internet sites, or magazine articles highlighting the 1920s (available at a public library or perhaps at your school library; also, see Internet sites with information at end of unit.)

- After completing research on that time period by using the student text, trade books, or Internet sites, each student will choose a hero from the 1920s. Each student must also decide on a hero of today. Then in pairs, they must plan two five-minute interviews between their heroes of the 1920s and their heroes of today. (Ex: Babe Ruth interviewing Britney Spears.) The partners must decide which hero they will be portraying in the interview. A script must be written with at least five questions for each celebrity.

- Present the interview to classmates and videotape the presentation of the celebrity interviews.

- Have the class view the taped interviews and complete a critique of each segment.

Strategies/Skills: Brainstorming, role-playing, analysis, boundary breaker

Primary *LTM* component: *Interpersonal Communication, Problem Solving*

LESSON 5

Women of the 1920s

- Students will complete research on women's roles in the 1920s. They can use the student text, trade books, Internet sites, or other sources to gather data. Discuss the differences between women in that time period and women of today. If time permits, students could have a short debate concerning whether it was better being a woman living in the '20s or a woman living today. Consider such issues as career, health, family life, and so on.

- Imagine you are a twenty-five-year-old mother of six, working in a factory in the early 1900s. What might your life be like? What if you were magically transported to the year 2001? In what ways might your everyday life be changed?

- Divide into pairs. Each pair will read an article found on the Internet, such as *Flapper Jane* or *Women Must Learn to Play the Game as Men Do* (referenced at end of unit). These articles can be preselected and bookmarked on computer by the teacher, or the students may search for articles themselves. Have students discuss the article with partners, and then answer the written analysis worksheet. (See sample at end of unit.) The pairs will then present their findings to the rest of the class.

- Take time to browse the section in the student text (determined by the school system) that focuses on women in the 1920s, or search for additional sites that will provide further insight into women in that time period.

- Groups of three will then work together to create cartoons about some aspect of women's lives in the 1920s. Each cartoon *must* use an analogy.

- Debrief on feelings about the lives of women in the 1920s. Have students research the term "flapper." Would you have wanted to be a "flapper" in that day? Why or why not?

- Explain that the next lesson will deal with advertising teams. Students will develop a new product and think of ways to market it. Assign teams of three and let them brainstorm a "new" product.

- On a piece of paper, answer this question: How was the life of a flapper different from that of her mother?

Strategies/Skills: Compare/contrast, analysis, analogy, role-playing

Primary *LTM* strategy: *Cognition*

LESSON 6

Advertising

- Brainstorm the effects that commercials, magazine ads, and newspaper ads have on people today. Explain that *credit* or the *installment plan* made buying easy in the 1920s. Have students complete some research on the economy in the 1920s.

- Divide students into market groups of three. Teams work together to create a new product. They may use any reference material to see what was "new" in the 1920s. The products of their advertising campaigns must be:

  a. a new product with a name (either created or drawn on paper)

  b. a forty-five-second radio commercial to advertise their product

  c. a full-page magazine ad

  d. a slogan or jingle for their product

- Have groups present their campaigns. Remind them that television commercials are not an option, as television had not yet been invented! The radio commercials will be audio-taped, and reviewed for feedback as to whether or not the audience could "see" the product through the medium of sound alone.

- Ask students to secretly vote on the best advertising campaign. If there is a clear winner, discuss why it was chosen. Were certain parts of each presentation more effective than others? Explain. Debrief the entire advertising campaign process.

- Begin a discussion on how the prosperity of the 1920s took a nosedive into the Depression years. Ask students to relate those events to the recent decline in the stock market. Is there a valid comparison?

Strategies/Skills: Brainstorming, cooperative learning

Primary *LTM* component: *Decision Making/Interpersonal Communication*

LESSON 7

Effects of the Great Depression on Family Life

- Show students selected portions of a videotape on some aspect of the Depression. One example is *The Story of Franklin Delano Roosevelt* (reference available at end of unit). Students should also research articles on the Internet dealing with growing up in the 1930s.

Some examples might include: *Growing Up White in the South in the 1930's* and *Growing Up Black in the 1930's in McCulley's Quarters, Alabama* (reference available at end of unit).

- Show a film on *The Great Depression*. Discuss content.

- Choose a partner and develop six interview questions that you will ask a classmate about growing up in the Twenty-First Century. Turn in your six questions. Then each group will draw a set of questions and interview his/her partner for the class. (Interviews will be tape recorded.)

- Working alone, create a political cartoon about the Depression years. (You may use symbols, analogies, or caricatures.)

- Have each student explain his/her cartoon. Display the cartoons in the classroom.

- As an assignment, have students conduct an interview with someone who lived during the Depression. Brainstorm five questions for use in the interview. The interview should be written or taped.

- At a later date, students should present the interviews they did with someone who lived during the Depression. An insightful discussion should follow the presentations as students come to realize what it was like to live during that time period.

Strategies/Skills: Creative writing, analogies, ethnographic interview, values education

Primary *LTM* strategy: *Problem Solving, Decision Making*

LESSON 8

Superheroes

- As a group, brainstorm: "What did people need during the Depression?" Most of the needs will likely be physical. If so, after a few minutes ask if there were any emotional or social needs. Then explain how the need for escape led to the creation of superhero comic books during the Depression. Let the students research the history of superheroes using trade books, the Internet, or other sources.

- Have students research superheroes (such as Captain America, Superman, and Batman), which were all created during the 1930s.

- In pairs, discuss how heroes and superheroes are alike and/or different. Make a list of these traits. Students should be able to separate/define "real heroes" from "superheroes."

- Still in pairs, brainstorm a list of problems people encounter today. Considering reasons why people created superheroes during the Depression years, students will create a superhero for today, attempting to solve one or more of the problems they have identified.

- Compare and contrast your superhero with the hero you picked from the '20s. Does your hero of the '20s fit your hero attributes? Are the two alike in any way?

- Plan a program for parents to see/hear the products created during this unit.

- We have seen a resurgence in popularity in superheroes. Recent movies such as *Spiderman, Xmen,* and *Daredevil* are examples. Compare and contrast the reasons why superheroes might me needed in today's society, just as they were needed during the Depression years.

Strategies/Skills: Compare/contrast, ethnographic interview

Primary *LTM* component: *Problem Solving*

Additional Teacher Information

Additional activities to extend and expand this unit are listed at the end of the unit.

LESSON 9

Images of the Depression

- Give each student a photo analysis worksheet. (Sample worksheet is at end of unit.) First, let the group discuss the questions on the sheet. Then show overhead transparencies of photographs that were taken during the Depression. (These can be gathered from the various Web sites listed at the end of this unit.) Discuss these Depression images. In pairs, students must answer the photo analysis questions after each image is shown.

- Tell students they may take two Polaroid pictures (black-and-white) of images they want to remember from the present. First ask them to consider what images they might choose and why. If possible, have a collection of Polaroid instant cameras available for the students to borrow. Or, ask the students to complete this project in teams over a weekend using personal cameras and black-and-white film.

- After they have taken the photos, have them share their images and explain why they might tell future generations about the time period in which we live.

- Ask students to imagine what a class in the year 2200 might find about the decade 2000–2010. Encourage creativity and insight into today's problems and issues. Share the book *Motel of the Mysteries* by David McCauley. This creative book details a humorous look at what might be discovered if future archaeologists were to discover a buried site from our current civilization.

- Final presentation to parents. Display of student products.

Strategies/Skills: Problem solving, analysis, oral presentation

Primary *LTM* component: *Interpersonal Communication*

FROM BABE RUTH TO BREADLINES
ACTIVITY RESOURCES

CARTOON ANALYSIS

A complete Cartoon Analysis Worksheet is available at http://www.nara.gov/education/teaching/analysis/cartoon.html.

If you are unable to access this site, a brief version follows:

1. List the objects or people you see in the cartoon.

   a. Identify the cartoon caption and/or title.

   b. Record important dates.

2. Which of the objects are symbols? What do these symbols mean?

   a. Which words or phrases are most significant? Why?

   b. List adjectives to describe the emotions portrayed in the cartoon.

3. Describe the action taking place.

4. Explain how the words clarify the symbols.

5. What special interest group would agree or disagree with cartoon's message? Explain.

SCAVENGER HUNT

A complete Scavenger Hunt is available on-line at http://cagle.slate.msn.com/teacher/elementary. If you are unable to access the site, a brief version as follows.

Find the following:

a donkey	a dollar bill	a baby
an elephant	an old man or woman	a soldier
a president	a gun	a skull and crossbones
a monument	a politician	a farm animal
a bird	Statue of Liberty	a flag
Uncle Sam	picket signs	garbage
a dove	a shark	a gravestone

WRITTEN DOCUMENT ANALYSIS WORKSHEET

A complete written document analysis worksheet is available on-line at http://nara.gov/education/ teaching/analysis/write.html. If you are unable to access the site, a modified version follows.

1. TYPE OF DOCUMENT

    __newspaper   __map   __advertisement

    __letter   __press release   __memo

2. UNIQUE PHYSICAL QUALITIES OF THE DOCUMENT

    __interesting letterhead   __handwritten

    __typed   __seals   __other

3. Date(s) of document:

4. Author (creator) of document:

5. For what audience was the document written?

6. List three things the author said that you think are important:

7. List two things the document tells you about life in the United States at the time it was written:

PHOTO ANALYSIS WORKSHEET

A complete photo analysis worksheet is available on-line at http://www.nara.gov /education/teaching/ analysis/photo.html. If you are unable to access the site, a modified version as follows:

1. Study the photograph for two minutes. Form an overall impression of the photograph and then examine individual items. Next, divide the photo into quadrants and study each section to see what new details become visible.

2. List people, objects, and activities in the photograph.

3. List three things that you might infer from this photograph.

4. What questions does this photograph raise in your mind?

5. Where could you find answers to them?

REFERENCES

Lesson 1

Castenson, Doug. "Exploring Cartooning." Available from http://edservices.aea7.k12.ia.us/edtech/teacherpages.

Lesson 3

Cagle, Peg. *Scavenger Hunt.* Professional Cartoon Index. Available from http://cagle.slate.msn. Educational Staff. 1998. *Cartoon Analysis Worksheet.* Washington, DC: National Archives and Records Administration. Available from www.nara.gov.

Lesson 4

Claycomb, Robert. (1973). *The great depression: Causes, effects, solutions.* Educational Audio Visual, Inc. Pleasantville, NY. 18 min. 15 sec. Sound filmstrip set.

Lesson 5

Bliven, Bruce. (1925). *Flapper Jane. The Americans.* McDougal Littell Inc., 1999.

Educational Staff. 1998. *Written document analysis worksheet.* Washington, DC: National Archives and Records Administration. Available from www.nara.gov.

Knower, Rosemary H. (1995). *Failure is impossible.* Upper Marlboro, MD: National Archives and Records Administration. Available from www.nara.gov.

Roosevelt, Eleanor. (1928). *Women must learn to play the game as men do. The Americans.* Geneva, IL: McDougal-Littell Inc., 1999.

Lesson 7

Johnson, Claudia Durt. "Interview: Growing Up Black in the 1930s In McCulleys Quarters, Alabama" from *Understanding To Kill A Mockingbird.* Available from http://library.thinkquest.org.

Johnson, Claudia Durt. "Interview: Growing Up White in the South in the 1930s" from *Understanding To Kill A Mockingbird.* Available from http://library.thinkquest.org.

Longoria, Sylvia R. 1998. *Great Depression Couldn't Defeat Holiday Spirit.* Corpus Christi: Corpus Christi *Times.* Available from longorias@scripps.com.

Questar Video Inc. 1941. *The story of Franklin Delano Roosevelt.* Produced by Hearst Entertainment. 100 min. Videocassette.

Lesson 8

Colville, Jamie. *The History of Superhero Comic Books.* Available from www.geocities.com.

Lesson 9

Educational Staff. 1998. *Photo Analysis Worksheet.* Washington, DC: National Archives and Records Administration. Available from www.nara.gov.

Library of Congress, Prints and Photographs Division, FSA-OWI Collection.

Parker, Jeanette Plauche. 1989. *Instructional Strategies for Teaching the Gifted.* Boston: Allyn and Bacon, Inc.

ADDITIONAL ACTIVITIES

Students may want to delve more deeply into the issues discussed in this unit. If time permits, students might complete some or all of the following discussion topics and activities:

- Psychologists tell us there are countless emotions expressed by human beings. Can emotions be expressed through cartooning? How?

- The Internet offers unlimited access to information on political (editorial) cartooning. Search for three active American political cartoonists. Find an example of each of their works.

- Theodor Geisel, better known as Dr. Seuss, is world famous for his children's books. An examination of his past, however, will reveal a strong connection to editorial cartoons. You'll be surprised!

- *Malapropisms* sound funny when other people use them. Do you know what they are? Can you find a locally printed cartoon that uses this type of humor?

- Ask a local artist to come to our class and help us with simple sketching techniques.

- Read a biography of Thomas Nast. Who was he, and why is he important?

- Who is your favorite cartoon character? Why did you choose this one?

- *Cartoon strips* and *cartoon panels* both show humor and wit. Their methods vary. What are the differences between cartoon strips and panel cartoons?

- Summarize the characteristics of a good editorial cartoon.

- If you wanted to find a Web site that would help you learn to draw cartoon figures, where would you go? After you have found three good drawing Web sites for students, share them with the class.

- Editorial cartooning is great entertainment for us. However, it serves a valuable function in our society. What is it?

- Do editorial cartoonists make good salaries? Find examples.

- Select a favorite editorial cartoonist, write a short biography, and turn in three different samples of his or her cartoon work.

- Joseph Keppler was important in the history of cartoons. Want to know why? Go to the school library and see if they have information on him. Better yet, try the Internet!

- I bet you'd never guess who is given credit for creating the oldest political cartoon?! Find out.

- Get information on Carl Schurz. Who is he, and why is he important?

- Cartoons are a big hit in Europe. Find and print examples of international cartoons. Have countries ever banned cartoons? Which countries, and why?

- Which cartoon character are you most like, and why? If you are not like any particular character, create one that is more like you.

- Editorial cartoons attract the most attention when they are simple. Sometimes one word or one symbol sends a powerful message. Create a cartoon using only one symbol or one word.

- Find out how your local newspaper chooses its editorial cartoons.

- Brainstorm a controversial local issue with someone else in class, and develop a cartoon using that topic. Try to use an analogy for your theme.

- Create your very own trademark cartoon character. Let this Mr. Know-It-All be the spokesman for your cartoons.

- Set up a cartoon display area within the classroom and post original cartoons from at least three other students.
- Create an original cartoon using Adobe Photoshop.
- You have forty-five minutes of class time to teach the history of political cartooning. You will be teaching a group of twenty-five seniors. How would you do it?
- Using newspapers or magazines, find three cartoons about Election 2000 and analyze their meanings.
- Publish an original article on editorial cartooning in the school newspaper.
- Learn to use a software program for cartooning.
- Convince a local newspaper to print one of your original cartoons.
- Teach another class at your school how to create editorial cartoons.
- Start a cartooning club at your school.
- Set up a cartoon Web site for your class.

INTERNET SITES OF INTEREST

Editorial Cartoon Bingo
http://cagle.slate.msn.com/teacher/high/lessonplanHS3.asp

Cartoon Scavenger Hunt
http://cagle.slate.msn.com/teacher/high/lessonplanHS4.asp

Cartoon News Magazine
http://cartoonews.com

Expressing Emotions through Cartoons
http://web2.infotrac.galegroup.com

Teacher's Guide to Professional Cartoonists Index Web Site
http://cagle/slate.msn.com/teacher/

Teacher's Guide to Current Events
http://cagle.slate.msn.com/teacher/high/lessonplanHS1.asp

Teacher's Guide to Forming Opinions
http://cagle.slate.msn.com/teacher/high/lessonplanHS2.asp

Classroom Activity—"Toons Talk to the Issue"
http://www.justthink.org

Middle School Lesson: Political Cartoons
http://ali.apple.com/edres/mslessons/polcartoon.shtml

Using Cartoons to Teach About Elections Past and Present
http://www.education-world.com/a_curr/curr210shtml

Writing Prompts: Political Cartoons (Writing across the Social Studies Curriculum)
http://www.indiana.edu/~eric_rec/bks/wacsocex.html

Political Cartoons and Cartoonists
http://www.boondocksnet.com/gallery/pc_intro.html

A Brief History of Political Cartoons
http://xroads.virginia.edu/~MA96/PUCK/part1.html

Interpreting Political Cartoons
http://yn.la.ca.us/

Exploring Cartooning by Doug Castenson
http://edservices.aea7.k12.ia.us/edtech/teacherpages/dcastenson

Political Cartoons (The Emma Goldman Papers)
http://sunsite.berkeley.edu/Goldman/Curricula/FreeExpression

Chapter Ten

Shakin' Up Shakespeare: The Life and Times of a Great Playwright and Poet

Originated by Barbara Begnaud

Subject Area: Social Studies and Language Arts

Grade Levels: 6–12

OVERVIEW AND RATIONALE

The purpose of this unit is twofold. It was designed to a) excite students' learning about Shakespeare before and during experiencing his works in a regular language arts curriculum, and b) calm their inhibitions toward what many consider difficult language and subject matter. Students are invited to learn about the Elizabethan era in which Shakespeare lived and to relate their knowledge to modern-day problems and issues. They are also encouraged to discover the way in which Shakespeare wrote in order to develop an understanding of the meanings of his plays and sonnets. This unit plan was developed not to have students read entire Shakespearian works, but to have them become familiar with the subject matter that Shakespeare broached: love, hate, trust, betrayal, the human struggle for power, comedy, tragedy, and family relationships.

Shakespeare lives on in movies, novels, music, and speeches, both political and personal. The premise is for students to understand how and why many of Shakespeare's quotes and ideas are still used today. Students will use a variety of cognitive, problem solving, writing, and creativity strategies to introduce them to Shakespeare and to help them understand that Shakespeare isn't "so scary!"

UNIT GOALS

- To investigate and become familiar with Elizabethan language, costumes, architecture, government, trade and labor, art, and so on and put research into organized, meaningful segments using timelines, Venn diagrams, and graphic organizers

- To develop an understanding of why Shakespeare is so important in literature and to instill an appreciation for his works

- To synthesize and put to use the knowledge that has been acquired by relating it to modern times

- To identify biographical information on the Elizabethan period's most famous writer, William Shakespeare, and to create artifacts and complete projects relating to his life and times

Shakin' Up Shakespeare *LTM* Activities

Cognition Activities:	*Interpersonal Communication* Activities:
• Shakesin' it up • Go Global • Will Shakespeare WHAT?	• It's all relative • Dr. Seusspeare • To thine own self be new
Leadership Training Model	
Problem Solving Activities:	*Decision Making* Activities:
• Poetry in commotion • Methinks it's time to party!	• And they all lived happily ever after . . . or not • Commercializing on Shakespeare

LESSON 1

Shakesin' It Up

- Students will begin thinking about great literary minds by brainstorming some of the most famous authors, playwrights, poets, and journalists they can think of. The teacher will start the discussion by contributing examples such as Marlowe, Longfellow, and Thoreau, or Grisham, Rice, King, or even Dr. Seuss. Encourage students to identify particular works with the literary figures who wrote them. Students may identify *Faustus* with Marlowe or *Hop on Pop* with Dr. Seuss. When students reach an adequate number of literary personalities, the teacher will introduce them to the fact that the class will be studying William Shakespeare and the Elizabethan period in depth.

- Students will be given an acrostic poem template with the name SHAKESPEARE written vertically down the page. (See sample at end of unit.) Each student is to complete his or her poem based on the knowledge that they already have, which may not be extensive. Therefore the words scary or sensitive for S or other generalizations are acceptable for this poem. Students will share their work, and a discussion may ensue regarding the words they chose to fit each letter of Shakespeare's name. For example, why is Shakespeare considered scary (S) or persuasive (P)? This will allow students to piggyback off of each other.

- From the discussion, students will use resource material, Internet resources, books, movies, and other sources to learn about the man who was William Shakespeare and the time in which he lived, the Elizabethan period. Students should be encouraged to discover what important events were occurring at the time of Shakespeare's birth and death, and during the course of his life. Students will discuss their findings with classmates.

- Students will construct a timeline of events surrounding Shakespeare. They may choose to do this activity in a variety of ways.

  They may write an historical account

  They may write out a time line or a word web

  They may use artistic talents to draw certain events

  They may record an oral history

- Finally, students will complete a graphic organizer asking them to choose the seven most important facts or features of William Shakespeare's life. Students are encouraged to use drawings, magazine pictures, and other colorful devices, which will aid in their recall of these events.

- Summarize the activity and ask students to discuss with their parents, which, if any, of Shakespeare's plays they have read or famous lines they may remember from a particular play. Students may even ask their parents to complete the acrostic poem presented earlier in the lesson.

Strategies/Skills: Accessing prior knowledge, research

Primary *LTM* component: *Cognition*

LESSON 2

And They All Lived Happily Ever After . . . Or Not

- The teacher will introduce some of Shakespeare's most popular works by securing copies of several Shakespearean works as well as abbreviated versions of his plays along with a list of all thirty-eight of his works. These are easily found on the Internet at http://shakespeare.palomar.edu. (Also see end of unit appendix for quick reference.) Share with students the general points of several selected plays, but be sure to read portions of them so that they may grasp the language used. The teacher may also choose to show the entirety of sections of movies like *Shakespeare in Love, Hamlet, Romeo & Juliet,* or *Macbeth.*

- Students will be asked to think about Shakespeare's plays in terms of tragedy and comedy. Assist students by referencing examples of modern stories they are familiar with that would fit into these two categories. Students should discuss implications, qualities, and similarities of the modern tale with the Shakespearean tale. They will be asked to complete a Venn diagram, labeling similarities and differences between tragedy and comedy. Students will then be asked to select a Shakespearean work, either comedy or tragedy, and change the ending so that it becomes the opposite of the way it was originally written. For example, they may decide that *Hamlet* should have a happy ending or *Much Ado About Nothing* may end with sadness. Students may choose to simply write out their new plays, or they may recruit classmates to act out their new endings.

- Students are encouraged to share their work and discuss why Shakespeare may have written a comedy instead of a tragedy, what influences were present in his life when he was writing each play, and/or what could have happened to make him, for example, let Romeo and Juliet live happily ever after or keep Beatrice and Benedick *(Much Ado About Nothing)* apart.

- Summarize the lesson by having each student share an "I learned" by describing what new information they may have learned in the lesson.

- For homework, students should brainstorm and select a fairly recent current event of interest to them, perhaps an environmental issue, poverty, illness, a scandal, politics, or the like. They should familiarize themselves with the event they choose.

- Challenge: What does the bubonic plague have to do with Shakespeare writing poetry instead of plays for two years? (See abbreviated history.)

Strategies/Skills: Brainstorming, creative writing

Primary *LTM* component: *Decision Making*

LESSON 3

Poetry in Commotion

- The teacher may begin by discussing the challenge question given during the last lesson.
- The lesson will begin with a reading of one of Shakespeare's sonnets. This would be a good time to remind students that Shakespeare was not only a playwright, but also a poet. Had it not been for the bubonic plague, the world might not ever have known Shakespeare as a poet. The lesson will develop as the teacher describes the components of a sonnet: a fourteen-line, rhyming poem in iambic pentameter. (Each line has ten syllables with alternating syllables stressed.) Shakespearean sonnets use an abab cdcd efef gg rhyming pattern. Students should discover which came first, Shakespeare or iambic pentameter, and whether Shakespeare was aware that he was writing in this style.
- Students will consider the current event they have selected. They will rewrite the event as a sonnet. Encourage students to use factual information about the event as well as their opinion of it. Students should attempt, however, to be ambiguous about the actual subject matter of their sonnet. For example, they should not use the actual names of people or corporations. (See sample poem at end of unit.)
- As students share their work, other students may attempt to guess the current event referenced in the sonnet.
- Students may then begin a discussion about other events, either current or historical, that interest them or that they would like to know more about. Record these occurrences for use in the next lesson.
- Summarize the lesson by having students tell something they have learned in iambic pentameter or in a rhyming pattern such as abab cdcd. For example:

> During the Gulf War we fought with Iraq
> And poems can result from such an attack.

Strategies/Skills: Synectics, creative writing

Primary *LTM* component: *Problem Solving*

LESSON 4

It's All Relative

- Students will begin the activity by recording a list of important national, international, current, and historical events. As a result of some emotional and important events being discussed, debates may arise. Encourage students to debate their opinions on issues, to ask questions, and to tie in events of Shakespeare's day. An example would be gender issues. Why were women not allowed to act in the theaters and how would things have been different if they had been able to? Do we still face issues such as those taking place when Shakespeare was alive? What can we do to resolve these issues?
- Have students choose events in history and compare them to Shakespeare's plays. Students may complete this portion of the activity individually or in groups. Group work may increase background knowledge about both the plays and the events, however, students should be encouraged to formulate their own ideas and opinions for the next portion of the activity in order to allow them to incorporate thoughts and ideas that are solely theirs, ones uninfluenced by their peers.

- Students will create a chart correlating major events to a Shakespearean theme. (See example at end of unit.)

- A Venn diagram may also be completed to compare and contrast movie versions of Shakespearean works to the actual play, if the teacher chooses to read an entire work with the class and to show an entire movie. It may also be used to compare the Elizabethan monarchy to the current one. The teacher should use a Venn diagram and allow students to choose and complete one of the above projects.

- Conclude the lesson by reviewing some of the events discussed and explaining that many things are just as important today as they were in the Elizabethan period. All things are relative, thus, the concept that history repeats itself and/or that some things never change! Ask students to look into their own past to recall stories by another famous author whom they have probably all read—Dr. Seuss. Students may even want to bring some examples from home!

Strategies/Skills: Small group discussion, debate, synetics, Venn diagrams

Primary *LTM* component: *Interpersonal Communication*

LESSON 5

Dr. Seusspeare

- The teacher should secure copies of several Dr. Seuss books. Begin the lesson with a brainstorm of several of Dr. Seuss's most famous works. The teacher will then read and distribute or post a copy of the poem "Green Eggs and Hamlet" included at the end of this unit and found at http://www.smsu.edu/English/eirc/shpag.html.

- Students will then summarize one of Shakespeare's plays in Dr. Seuss's rhyming style. Students should be as creative and clever as possible with titles, vocabulary, rhyme scheme, and other elements.

- When all poems are complete, students may work as a group to create a folio for their work. Individual students may choose to be publishers, illustrators, cover designers, photographers, or book jacket writers, with every student playing a role in completing the folio. Copies may be made and sent home with students, and a copy may be delivered to other teachers and administrators, and to the school or local library.

- Summarize the lesson and encourage students to spend some time watching television commercials and listening to radio ads and jingles in preparation for the next lesson. Be on the lookout for a topic, jingle, or message that might be "Shakespearean."

Strategies/Skills: Synetics, collaboration, creative writing, authentic purpose

Primary *LTM* component: *Interpersonal Communication*

LESSON 6

Commercializing on Shakespeare

- The teacher will begin the lesson by having students pick an ordinary household item out of a bag or a large box. See a list of items that may work well and several examples at the end of this unit. The student wil then make a brief list of the features and/or attributes of the product.

- Each student will be given a copy of famous Shakespearean quotes (http://www.allshakespeare.com/quotes/) to use in conjunction with the activity. One large copy of the quotes may be displayed on poster-board or on an overhead projector.

- Students will then write a commercial for television or radio using Shakespearean language, quotes, puns, and so forth. The item may be marketed as though it could be used in Shakespeare's world, or it may be simply a clever take on a quote. For example, the commercial for a bottle of stain remover could include Macbeth's famous "Out, damned spot! Out I say!"

- Students will act out their commercials for fellow students. They may also ask classmates for assistance in acting. The commercials may be recorded on a video camera or tape recorder for use in other classrooms, or the recording may even be sent to a manufacturer to give their marketing team some new ideas!

- Students will begin a recall activity using the alphabet. Recall As from the unit—anon, alas, Bs—bard, bubonic plague. Notify students that the reason for the recall session is that because over the next several lessons, students will use much of the information they have learned to collaborate and complete group projects.

Strategies/Skills: Lateral thinking, role play

Primary *LTM* component: *Decision Making*

LESSON 7

A Sign of the Times/To Thine Own Self Be New

Part I—A Sign of the Times

- Students will begin the activity by brainstorming parts of the newspaper—main news (national and international), birth announcements, weddings, obituaries, local news, sports, entertainment, comics, and so on. They will then make a list of some of the events they had discussed in past activities, which had happened during the Elizabethan period—the births of Christopher Marlowe and Galileo, the beheading of Mary, Queen of Scots, the formation of the East India Company, and the defeat of the Spanish Armada. For quick reference, a time line can be found at http://shakespeare.palomar.edu/timeline/summarychart.htm.

- Students will begin writing newspaper articles, drawing political cartoons, writing comics, designing advertising, and so forth to describe some of these historical events. If they are in need of language help, a glossary of Shakespearean words may be found at http://shakespeare.palomar.edu/life.htm#History.

- The newspaper, *The Shakespearean Times,* or whatever students choose to call their own paper, will be edited, formatted, and distributed to teachers, students, and others.

Part II—To Thine Own Self be New

- Students will be introduced to the concept that for many years, it was believed that there was actually not a man named William Shakespeare, that the name was a pen name for another writer of the time. Another belief is that the writings are actually the work of several authors. The teacher may also introduce other authors who used pen names. For example, Samuel Clemens used the pen name Mark Twain, which is a reference to a depth measure along the river. Have students research famous authors who changed their names or used other names when writing in different styles or genres.

- Students may then come up with a pen name for themselves and may use this name as the byline for their newspaper article or cartoon.
- Review the activity and tell the students that in the next lesson they will take a trip around Shakespeare's Globe!

Strategies/Skills: Brainstorming, creative writing, originality

Primary *LTM* component: *Interpersonal Communication*

LESSON 8

Go Global!

- The teacher should secure a list of the complete works of Shakespeare. Students will research the setting for each play. For example, *Hamlet* was set in Denmark, and *Romeo and Juliet* in Italy.
- Students will use a large world map to mark the location of each of the plays. Each student will design an icon to designate some reference to the play. For example, the student who determines that *Romeo and Juliet* took place in fair Verona may design a star-crossed lovers icon for the map.
- Students will construct a map of what they think London may have looked like during Shakespeare's time based on their research. Students may hand draw their map, make a three-dimensional map out of clay, cut out pictures from magazines, build models of buildings, or use other supplies to designate rivers, mountains, roads, and other features. Students may also choose to design a map of Hamlet's Denmark, Romeo and Juliet's Italy, or even Shakespeare's hometown of Stratford-upon-Avon. Have students share their products.

Strategies/Skills: Research, prior knowledge, mapmaking

Primary *LTM* component: *Cognition*

LESSON 9

Will Shakespeare. Will Shakespeare What?

- The teacher should secure a copy of William Shakespeare's Last Will and Testament (http://fly.hiwaay.net/~paul/shakspere/shakwill.htm). The language in the will is particularly difficult, so as the group reads it, a list of items and to whom they were given should be made.
- Students will then individually rewrite Shakespeare's will, leaving his possessions to modern figures. For example: I leave my sword to Mike Tyson, not that he needs another excuse to get violent, but if he's going to remove people's ears, he should at least be prepared.
- Students will then be taught to make a quill pen from a feather (*Shakespeare for Kids* has a good method and gives a description) and the strokes of basic calligraphy. They will also make a scroll look antiqued. This is easily done by dabbing heavy paper with tea bags.
- Students will practice writing their own copy of the revised will before writing a final draft on the dry antiqued paper using their quill pen and calligraphy. The movie *Shakespeare in Love* gives an interesting version of how Shakespeare physically wrote his plays.

- Students will begin reviewing information they have learned about Shakespeare and the Elizabethan period. Hang poster paper or butcher paper on the walls of the classroom and allow students to write things that they have learned, their favorite attributes of Shakespeare, favorite quotes, and so on.

- Advise students that the next activity will be the culminating project and that they should be getting excited about an end-of-the-unit party!

Strategies/Skills: Synectics, creative writing

Primary *LTM* component: *Cognition*

SHAKESPEARE CULMINATING ACTIVITY

Methinks It's Time to Party!

- Using the knowledge they have gained in this unit, students will plan a Shakespearean/Elizabethan festival.

  Students will plan and create:

Invitations	Decorations
Music	Games/entertainment
Food	Art displays
Costumes	

- Some students will narrate a brief oral history of the Elizabethan period and role-play scenes from Shakespearean plays.
- Some students will speak using Shakespearean language.
- Some students will demonstrate what some artisans may have done for careers.
- Students will end the day with games, music, and art from this particularly interesting and dynamic time in history. The teacher may also want to have a poster with the acrostic poem from Lesson 1 reprinted to hang on the wall with markers nearby. During the party, students may want to add their new knowledge to the poem.

Strategies/Skills: Collaboration, synthesis, creative dramatics, creative writing

Primary *LTM* component: *Interpersonal Communication*

EXTENDED ACTIVITIES

Potpourri and Potent Quotables

- Students will create and play a Jeopardy game and test their knowledge of Shakespeare, his plays and characters, and the Elizabethan period (Students may come up with their own questions in addition to the ones listed at the end of this unit.)

Shakespeare, Rattle & Roll

- Write a song to the tune of a modern-day hit based on a Shakespearean play.

I'm Not a Moron and Don't Call Me Oxy

- Study and find oxymorons as found in Shakespeare's plays and come up with a few of your own (for example: Without eyes . . . see [Romeo]).
- Students may also study and find alliteration, simile, hyperbole, personification.

Lights, Camera, Action

- Act out some scenes from Shakespeare's plays.

Shakespearean Careerean

- Determine some careers that may have been prevalent in the Elizabethan period, find evidence of them in Shakespeare's plays, and relate it to a modern career.

For Medicinal Purposes Only

- Students may make a pomander ball to keep the plague away or plant an herb garden as a remedy for common illnesses of the Elizabethan period.

Speaking of Shakespeare

- Students will practice speaking Old English.

What's in A Name?

- Students will design a family coat of arms.

You can Quote Me on That!

- Students will keep a quote journal of their favorite quotes and their meanings.

Draw Your Sword, Sir!

- Students will study and practice the art of fencing.

You can Build the World

- No, just The Globe! Students will build a replica of The Globe Theater, perhaps add puppets, and role-play one of Shakespeare's works on the stage.

Ready, Set, Go

- Students will design and build sets from scenes from Shakespeare's plays.

Across the Curriculum

- Students will complete the crossword puzzle found at http://student.ccbc.cc.md.us/~cminnier/puzzles/plays.htm.

ABBREVIATED HISTORICAL INFORMATION FOR SHAKIN' UP SHAKESPEARE: THE LIFE AND TIMES OF A GREAT PLAYWRIGHT AND POET

The reign of Queen Elizabeth I marks an incredible renaissance in English history, one that had begun in Italy over 100 years earlier. At the age of twenty-five, Elizabeth gained control of the country and reigned for forty-five years, thus the second half of the sixteenth century is duly named the Elizabethan period.

Elizabeth was the daughter of Henry VIII and Anne Boleyn, and was actually third in line for the throne, behind half-brother Edward (who died at age fifteen) and half-sister Mary (Bloody Mary, whose zealous plot to re-Catholicize the nation brought about a true reign of terror). Her commitment to art, literature, and philosophy gave playwrights such as William Shakespeare and Christopher Marlowe (of *Dr. Faustus* fame, who was born the same year as Shakespeare) the opportunity to perform for the court as well as to be patronized by it.

The class system was in full effect; however, almost everyone experienced the cultural awakening developed under Elizabeth's monarchy. Although the bubonic plague haunted much of Elizabeth's time as queen, highlights of her reign include the defeat of the Spanish Armada, Drake's Second Circumnavigation of the Globe, the birth of Galileo, and the push toward colonization with the formation of the East India Company. Two universities, Oxford and Cambridge, were also recognized and dubbed as centers for "learning and scholarly endeavor." (Peters) Elizabeth remained throughout the majority of her time as queen (with the exception of the threat of rebellion in the late 1590s), a steadfast and well-suited leader.

William Shakespeare was born to John and Mary Arden Shakespeare in 1564 in Stratford-upon-Avon. In the year of his birth, eighty thousand people died of the bubonic plague. The plague was caused by an overabundance of garbage, rats, and fleas; however, since many believed the foul-smelling air was the culprit, they were prone to growing herbs and fruits or smelling pomander balls.

Stargazers have said that William was born under a rhyming planet. After probable attendance at King Edward VI's New School, he married Anne Hathaway (eight years his senior and three months pregnant at the time) and sired three children—Susanna in 1583 and twins Hamnet and Judith two years later. At age twenty-two, he left for London for reasons unknown. Only ten years before Shakespeare's arrival in London had acting become a legalized profession. It is unclear exactly when Shakespeare began working as either playwright or actor in the theaters, but by 1592, he had assuredly read *Chronicles of England, Scotland and Ireland* and written several plays, including *Henry VI, Parts I, II and III*.

The plagues forced the closure of the theaters for nearly two years. During these years, Shakespeare turned to writing poems and sonnets. Soon enough, though, in 1594, the theaters were reopened and Shakespeare became a "sharer" in the Lord Chamberlain's Men, a group of players for whom he was the prized writer. After the death of his son Hamnet, Shakespeare, along with the Lord Chamberlain's Men, rebuilt The Theater on the other side of the Thames in Southwark. They named it The Globe. As owners, they shared a larger profit, and William bought the second-largest home in the city of London, as well as a cottage and some land in Stratford. Commoners as well as nobles came from far and wide to see Shakespeare's plays performed at The Globe. Three thousand people at a time packed the playhouse.

Elizabeth I died in 1603 after a forty-five-year reign over England, leaving James VI of Scotland, or James I, as he became known in England, to the throne. Because of their success, the Lord Chamberlain's Men became known as the King's Men and performed regularly for the court. In 1611, Shakespeare returned to Stratford-upon-Avon to live out the remainder of his days, journeying back to London on

SHAKIN' UP SHAKESPEARE (Continued)

only a few select occasions. While Shakespeare was in Stratford, a cannon blast in the fourth scene of *Henry VIII* caused The Globe in London to catch fire. No one was injured and all of Shakespeare's plays were rescued from the fire, but as far as historians can tell, he never wrote another play. The Globe was rebuilt and remained intact until 1644, when it was torn down as a result of the English Civil War. However, in 1970, an American undertook the project of rebuilding the theater near its original site, and The Globe has stood there since its completion in 1995.

Before his death on April 23, 1616, Shakespeare completed thirty-eight plays and many poems and sonnets. He was buried at Holy Trinity Church in Stratford, England. The *First Folio,* a collection of thirty-six of his thirty-eight plays, was gathered by John Heminges and Henry Condell and printed around 1623. The forward by friend and fellow poet Ben Jonson reads; "He was not a man of an age, but for all time." Indeed, Shakespeare's words and works have continued to inspire people for over four centuries and will surely continue to have an impact on generations to come.

The above information was collected from the following sources:

Aagesen, C. and Blumberg, M. (1999). *Shakespeare for Kids: His Life and Times: 21 Activities.* Chicago: Chicago Review Press.

Peters, M. *Elizabeth I and the Elizabethan Period: A Brief Introduction.* Available at http://www.springfield.k12.il.us/schools/springfield/eliz/index.html

SHAKESPEARE JEOPARDY QUESTIONS

Potent Quoteables: Who said the following famous quote?

1. To be or not to be, that is the question (Polonius)
2. Et tu, Brute (Julius Caesar)
3. Out damned spot, out, I say! (Lady Macbeth)
4. Good night! Good night! Parting is such sweet sorrow! (Juliet)
5. Friends, Romans, Countrymen. Lend me your ears! (Mark Antony)
6. The lady doth protest too much, methinks (Queen Gertrude, Hamlet)
7. Now is the Winter of our discontent (Richard III)
8. I have no other but a woman's reason (Lucetta, Two Gentlemen of Verona)
9. Get thee to a nunn'ry (Hamlet)
10. I am a Jew, Hath a Jew not eyes (Shylock, Merchant of Venice)

Biographical Sketch

1. Year of Shakespeare's birth (1564)
2. Queen during most of Shakespeare's life (Elizabeth I)
3. Shakespeare's wife (Anne Hathaway)
4. Shakespeare's only son (Hamnet)
5. Profession of Shakespeare's father (glove maker)
6. River on which Shakespeare was born (Avon)

7. Theater company for which Shakespeare performed (Lord Chamberlain's Men)
8. That company later became known as (The King's Men)
9. Age at which Shakespeare left Stratford (twenty-two)
10. Church at which Shakespeare is buried (Holy Trinity)

World Events

1. During Shakespeare's life Hawkins journeyed to the New World for the__ time (second)
2. Christopher Marlowe was killed in this type of brawl (barroom)
3. This sailor circumnavigated the globe for the second time (Drake)
4. This scientist was born the same year as Shakespeare (Galileo)
5. Of *Dr. Faustus* fame, this author was also born the same year as Shakespeare (Marlowe)
6. This plague ran rampant during much of the Elizabethan age (bubonic)
7. This Naval Fleet was destroyed by England in 1588 (Spanish Armada)
8. This former queen was executed for treason during Shakespeare's childhood (Bloody Mary, or Mary, Queen of Scots)
9. This religion's founder John died the year Shakespeare was born (Calvinism)
10. Friend and fellow poet who wrote the introduction to Shakespeare's *First Folio* (Ben Jonson)

Elizabethan England

1. Elizabeth's half-brother who died at age fifteen (Edward)
2. Elizabeth's half-sister who reigned for a short time (Mary)
3. Elizabeth's mother, second wife of Henry VIII (Anne Boleyn)
4. James VI of Scotland became this name when he replaced Elizabeth in 1603 (James I)
5. This was thought to cause the bubonic plague (foul-smelling air)
6. One of the two universities reorganized during Elizabeth's reign (Cambridge/Oxford)
7. Age at which Elizabeth took the throne of England (twenty-five)
8. Number of years Elizabeth reigned (forty-five)
9. The second half of this century is referred to as the Elizabethan period (sixteenth)
10. Family name of Elizabeth's monarch (Tudor)

All the King's Men

1. Title of the man who sponsored Shakespeare's players (Lord)
2. Original theater for which Shakespeare wrote (The Theatre)
3. Owner of twenty-one-year lease on original theater (Burbage)
4. Reason for Will's change to poetry (plague)
5. Reason for first destruction of The Globe (fire)

---

6. Reason for second destruction of The Globe (English Civil War)

7. The original company was renamed the King's Men when James I came into power (Lord Chamberlain's Men)

8. Religion that wanted an end to theater (Puritan)

9. Spenser's ode to Elizabeth was titled (The Faerie Queen)

10. Complete number of sonnets of Shakespeare, which equals to three times his plays plus forty (154)

Family Feud

1. Romeo's family name (Montague)

2. Juliet's family name (Capulet)

3. Juliet's cousin, whom Romeo killed (Tybalt)

4. Juliet's cause of death (dagger)

5. Where we lay our scene (Fair Verona)

6. Played Romeo in Baz Luhrman's version of *Romeo and Juliet* (Leonardo DeCaprio)

7. What light through this breaks (yonder window)

8. Speaker of Drawn in sword and talk of Peace (Tybalt)

9. A_____ o' both your houses (plague)

10. First meeting place of the star-crossed lovers (Capulet party)

Movie Madness

1. Mel Gibson's famous Dane (Hamlet)

2. Natalie Wood starred in this musical version of *Romeo and Juliet* (*West Side Story*)

3. Claire Danes played a_____ in Baz Luhrman's version of *Romeo and Juliet* (Capulet)

4. Shakespeare was mentioned in this Robin Williams boarding school flick (*Dead Poets Society*)

5. Hugh Grant read Shakespeare's sonnets to Kate Winslet in this English drama (*Sense and Sensibility*)

6. Liz Taylor starred in this Shakespeare classic (*Taming of the Shrew*)

7. This musical comedy was based on *Taming of the Shrew* (*Kiss Me Kate*)

8. Emma Thompson played Beatrice in this Shakespeare romantic comedy (*Much Ado About Nothing*)

9. Best picture in 1998 (*Shakespeare in Love*)

10. This Robin Williams film draws its title from *Hamlet* (*What Dreams May Come*)

Potpourri

1. Puck's Play (*Midsummer Night's Dream*)

2. Ophelia's father (Polonius)

---

3. Macbeth's title (Thane of Corder)
4. Benedick was Beatrice's love in which comedy? (*Much Ado About Nothing*)
5. Mark Antony made a famous speech to which groups? (Friends, Romans, Countrymen)
6. Elizabeth's reign brought about something that had happened in Italy 100 years earlier (Renaissance)
7. Nationality of the man who rebuilt The Globe in the 1970s (American)
8. Book from which Shakespeare wrote his histories (*Chronicles of England, Scotland and Ireland*)
9. Play during which The Globe burned down (*Henry VIII*)
10. Hamlet's country of origin (Denmark)

SHAKESPEARE'S PLAYS

Histories	Tragedies	Comedies	Poetry/Sonnets
Henry VI, Part 2	*Titus Andronicus*	*The Two Gentlemen of Verona*	"Venus and Adonis"
Henry VI, Part 3	*Romeo and Juliet*	*The Taming of the Shrew*	"The Rape of Lucrece"
Henry VI, Part 1	*Julius Caesar*	*The Comedy of Errors*	"A Lover's Complaint"
Richard III	*Hamlet*	*Love's Labours Lost*	"The Passionate Pilgrim"
Richard II	*Othello*	*A Midsummer Night's Dream*	"The Phoenix and The Turtle"
King John	*Timon of Athens*	*The Merchant of Venice*	
Henry IV, Part 1	*King Lear*	*The Merry Wives of Windsor*	
Henry IV, Part 2	*Macbeth*	*Much Ado About Nothing*	
Henry V	*Antony and Cleopatra*	*As You Like It*	
Henry VIII	*Coriolanus*	*Twelfth Night*	
		All's Well That Ends Well	

GREEN EGGS AND HAMLET

I ask to be or not to be
That is the question I ask of me.
This sullied life, it makes me shudder.
My uncle's boffing dear, sweet mother.
Would I, could I take me life?
Could I, should I end this strife?
Should I jump out of a plane?
Or throw myself before a train?
Should I from a cliff just leap?
Could I put myself to sleep?
Shoot myself or take some poison?
Maybe try self-immolation?
To shuffle off this mortal coil,
I could stab myself with a fencing foil.
Slash my wrists while in the bath?
Would it end my angst and wrath?
To sleep, to dream, now there's the rub.
I could drop a toaster in my tub.
Would all be glad if I were dead?
Could I perhaps kill them instead?
Hmmm . . . This line of thought takes consideration.
For I'm the King . . .
. . . . . . .of procrastination. . . .

SAMPLE MOVIE LIST

Hamlet

Romeo and Juliet

Shakespeare in Love

Renaissance Man

Dead Poets Society

A Midsummer Night's Dream

Kiss Me Kate

The Taming of the Shrew

West Side Story

10 Things I Hate About You

Macbeth

Much Ado About Nothing

Sense and Sensibility

What Dreams May Come (draws its title from Hamlet)

Elizabeth

ACROSTIC POEM

Sonnets soothing to the heart
Happy endings
Apothecaries and aristocrats
Kings in castles
East and West all know of the playwright
Some fear his works
Particularly those who have not gotten to know them
Eager ears will listen closely
As each tale unfolds
Read rigorously and intently
Each of Shakespeare's thirty-eight plays

Chart

Shakespeare Play	Quote or Theme	Current Event
King Claudius (Hamlet)	"Oh villain, villain, smiling, damned villain"	Saddam Hussein
Macbeth	Greed	Enron/Worldcom
Richard III	"Now is the Winter of our discontent"	Israeli/Palestinian conflict
The Tempest	"All the infections that the sun sucks up From bogs, fens, flats, on Prosper fall, and make him By inch-meal a disease!"	West Nile Encephalitis; SARs
Romeo and Juliet (Montague/Capulet)	"What's in a name?"	Bush and Clinton families

PRODUCT SAMPLES FOR COMMERCIAL

Baking Soda—"Something rotten in the state of your refrigerator? Use . . ."

Sleeping Pills—"May angels take thee to thy rest with . . ."

Flowers—Florist—"That which we call a rose by any other word would smell as sweet"

Lightbulb—"But soft, what light through yonder window breaks?"

Facial Lotion—"O that I were a glove upon the hand That I might touch that cheek!"

Mouthwash—"If her breath were as terrible as her terminations, there would be no living near her . . ."

Toothpaste—"Do you have a blasting and scandalous breath? Use . . ."

Perfume—". . . and so perfumed that The winds were lovesick with them"

Candle—"O, she doth teach the torches to burn bright!"

Soap—"What? Will these hands n'er be clean? They will with . . ." or "Ever ready to come to you with clean hands . . ."

Diapers—"Oh, Bottom, thou art changed!"

Ruler—"Measure by measure . . ."

CURRENT EVENT SONNET

The deed done here is not such a "good thing"
By Martha, who wears the domestic crown.
You should have hung up when your phone did ring
To give you the tip that could bring you down.

What would you do with the extra dough?
Are the sales of your magazine slipping?
Insider trading is wrong, don't you know?
Your story has become simply gripping!

Will the queen of the kitchen be dethroned?
Bet you wish now you had never ImCloned!

SITES OF INTEREST

http://shakespeare.palomar.edu/—a great reference point with time lines, genealogy, and more.

http://www.allshakespeare.com/index.php—Shakespeare's most famous quotes and abbreviated versions of plays.

http://www.glenridge.org/macbeth/download.html—Macbeth Star Wars movie.

http://www.smsu.edu/English/eirc/shpag.html—a fun site with quizzes and little-known facts.

http://www.stratford-upon-avon.co.uk/index.htm—complete guide to Shakespeare's birthplace.

http://www.teachersfirst.com/autoframe.htm?http://renaissance.dm.net/compendium/home.html—the definitive source on Elizabethan England.

REFERENCES

Aagesen, C. and Blumberg, M. (1999). *Shakespeare for kids: His life and times: 21 activities.* Chicago: Chicago Review Press.

Gibson, R. (1998). *Teaching Shakespeare: A handbook for teachers.* United Kingdom: Cambridge University Press.

Gibson, R. and Field-Pickering, J. (1999). *Discovering Shakespeare's language: 150 stimulating activity sheets for student work.* United Kingdom: Cambridge University Press.

Gurr, A. (1996). *Playgoing in Shakespeare's London.* United Kingdom: Cambridge University Press.

Papp, J. and Kirkland, E. (1998). *Shakespeare alive.* New York: Bantam Books.

Peters, M. *Elizabeth I and the Elizabethan Period: a Brief Introduction.* Available at http://www.springfield.k12.il.us/schools/springfield/eliz/index.html

The NASA Moon Survival Task*

You are a crew member on a space ship that is scheduled to rendezvous with a mother ship on the lighted surface of the moon. Unfortunately, mechanical difficulties have forced your ship to crash-land on a spot some 100 miles from the rendezvous point. The rough landing damaged much of the equipment on board. Since you must reach the mother ship in order to survive, your group must select the most critical items to take on the 100-mile trip. Below are listed the 15 items left intact after landing. Your task is to rank them in terms of their importance to your mission. Place a "1" by the most important item, a "2" by the second most important, and so on.

_____ A.   Box of matches

_____ B.   Food concentrate

_____ C.   50 feet of nylon rope

_____ D.   Parachute silk

_____ E.   Portable heating unit

_____ F.   Two .45 caliber pistols

_____ G.   One case of dehydrated milk

_____ H.   Two 100-pound tanks of oxygen

_____ I.   Map of the moon's constellations

_____ J.   Life raft

_____ K.   Magnetic compass

_____ L.   5 gallons of water

_____ M.   Signal flares

_____ N.   First-aid kit with injection needles

_____ O.   Solar-powered FM receiver-transmitter

*The NASA Moon Survival Task is adapted from its original version with the permission of its author,
Dr. Jay Hall, of Teleometrics International, 1755 Woodstead Court,
The Woodlands, Texas 77380 (713-367-0060).

When all groups have completed the task (approximately 15-20 minutes), allow them to share their group ratings and explain the reasons for their responses. Then present the answers contributed by the Manned Spacecraft Center of NASA in Houston, Texas (included on the following page), and discuss.

After completing the moon simulation, make note of those science concepts that need reinforcement. For example, any individual or group who did not rank oxygen and water as 1 and 2, respectively, may need information on the lack of these substances on the moon and/or on their essential nature for survival. Others may need information on gravity, radiation, or other concepts related to space travel. Taking one concept at a time, generate problems whose solutions might help the learner understand the concept under study. Select one problem for attach and develop an inquiry lesson designed to strengthen students' comprehension of the necessary information.

SCORING KEY FOR NASA MOON SURVIVAL TASK

15	A.	Box of matches (little or no use on moon in absence of oxygen)
4	B.	Food concentrate (supply daily energy needs)
6	C.	50 feet of nylon rope (useful in tying injured, helpful in climbing)
8	D.	Parachute silk (protection against sun's rays)
13	E.	Portable heating unit (useful only if party landed on dark side)
11	F.	Two .45 caliber pistols (self-propulsion devices)
12	G.	One case of dehydrated milk (food, mixed with water for drinking)
1	H.	Two 100-pound tanks of oxygen (fills respiration requirement)
3	I.	Map of the moon's constellations (essential for navigation)
9	J.	Life raft (CO_2 bottles included with raft may be used for self-propulsion across chasms, etc.)
14	K.	Magnetic compass (no magnetized poles on moon, thus of no use)
2	L.	5 gallons of water (replenish loss from perspiration)
10	M.	Signal flares (distress call when within line of sight)
7	N.	First-aid kit with injection needles (oral pills or injection medicine)
5	O.	Solar-powered FM receiver transmitter (communication when in range of mother ship)

The Leadership Training Model
Unit Outline
COGNITION AND *PROBLEM SOLVING*
(LEFT-BRAIN FUNCTIONS)

UNIT:_____

COGNITION

Exploration (community resources such as field studies, guest speakers, mentors, and learning centers, and effective use of media)
TLW*:

Specialization (narrow the process from broad conceptual base; focus on a particular topic or problem, problem definition)
TLW:

Investigative Skill Training (provide research and other skills necessary for and appropriate to a topic or investigative problem)
TLW:

Research (prepare the students experientially for innovative and cognition-based leadership that is needed for lifelong acquisition of skills and information)
TLW:

*The Learner will

PROBLEM SOLVING

Six-Step Approach to Creative Problem Solving

Activities: brainstorming, futuristic problem solving, scientific method of problem solving, conflict resolution techniques

Problem Perception and Definition
TLW:

Incubation
TLW:

Creative Thinking
TLW:

Analysis
TLW:

Evaluation
TLW:

Implementation
TLW:

INTERPERSONAL COMMUNICATION AND DECISION MAKING (RIGHT-BRAIN FUNCTIONS)

INTERPERSONAL COMMUNICATION

Activities: etiquette, values, social skills, trust walk, broken squares, communication skills, parliamentary procedure, debate, public speaking

Self-Realization
TLW:

Empathy
TLW:

Cooperation
TLW:

Conflict Resolution
TLW:

DECISION MAKING

Activities: development of realistic goals, ability to organize and implement plans for meeting these goals, formative and summative evaluation, values education, role-playing, simulation, counseling, social action projects

Independence of Thought
TLW:

Self-Confidence
TLW:

Acceptance of Responsibility
TLW:

Task Commitment
TLW:

Moral Strength
TLW:

Index

About the Authors

Jeanette Plauché Parker is Professor of Education and Director of the Center for Gifted Education at the University of Louisiana at Lafayette. Since the 1970s she has been active in the field of gifted education, starting a district program for gifted children, chairing the Professional Development Division of the National Association for Gifted Children, and spearheading a project to develop national standards. Dr. Parker published a major graduate text, "Instructional Strategies for Teaching the Gifted" and more than forty other publications in the field. Her Leadership Training Model, initially published in 1983, forms the basis for the current book on leadership development.

Lucy Gremillion Begnaud is Assistant Professor of Education and Director of Teacher Clinical Experiences at the University of Louisiana at Lafayette, teaching graduate classes in gifted education. She was an elementary teacher for nineteen years, twelve of those in gifted education. Dr. Begnaud has presented at state, national, and international conferences, has served as a consultant for school systems across the country, and has published several articles.

DATE DUE

Demco, Inc. 38-293